As a journalist at the Tulsa Tribune, I interviewed Leon Russell a few times; once at his Los Angeles home and recording studio and in Tulsa, thanks in no small part to the support and friendship of the wondrous Emily Smith ("Sweet Emily," indeed). Like many who appreciate this enormously talented musician and songwriter, I hoped to read a Russell-written memoir some day. That day has finally come, thanks to his wife, Jan Bridges, and book editors Steve Todoroff and John Wooley. Steve has been unstoppable on all things Leon, for which I am profoundly grateful.

— **Ellis Widner**, *Style editor, Arkansas Democrat-Gazette*

D0984835

LEON RUSSELL

IN HIS OWN WORDS

(WITH A LITTLE HELP FROM HIS FRIENDS)

LEON RUSSELL

IN HIS OWN WORDS

(WITH A LITTLE HELP FROM HIS FRIENDS)

by

Leon Russell

Edited and Annotated by
Steve Todoroff and John Wooley

stevetodoroff**archives**®

Steve Todoroff Archives
P.O. Box 278
Barker, TX 77413

ISBN: 978-1-886518-03-2 (paperback)
978-1-886518-02-5 (hardcover)

Library of Congress Control Number: 2019938521

Cover photo by Jim McCrary. Used with permission.
Back cover photo by John Boydston. Used with permission.
Book design by Elena Reznikova, DTPerfect.com

Printed in the United States of America

This book is dedicated to the LeonLifers,
the devoted members of Leon's traveling fan base
who crisscrossed the globe to see their favorite rock star.
Their own exploits would make a great book.

The editors would like to thank the following "friends,"
both living and dead, who contributed or wrote stories about Leon,
helping to make his original thin but powerful autobiography
a more informative and entertaining read.

CHUCK BLACKWELL

JIM BLAZER

J.J. CALE

CHUCK FARMER

GERALD GOODWIN

JOANNE GORDON

JIM KARSTEIN

JIM KELTNER

GUY LOGSDON

JIMMY MANRY

JIMMY MARKHAM

PETER NICHOLLS

EMILY SMITH

DIANE SULLIVAN

BRIAN JAMES THOMPSON

JACK WESSEL

JOHNNY WILLIAMS

A special thanks to Leon's wife, Jan Bridges,
for allowing us to be a part of this book,
and for sharing it with Leon's legions of fans worldwide.

CONTENTS

PROLOGUE

THE LEON RUSSELL autobiographical material you are about to read first came into my possession in 1992, when Leon sent me the Word Document files for a proposed book, with an eye on possibly combining his material with my own research on his life and career—something I'd been doing, at that time, for more than a decade. He was signed to Virgin Records then and had just completed an album for that label, with Bruce Hornsby co-producing, titled *Anything Can Happen*. Sadly, Virgin Records was sold by co-founder Richard Branson to Thorn EMI in June, 1992. That British conglomerate promptly dropped the bottom third of Virgin's roster, which unfortunately included the recently signed Russell.

I was thrilled that Leon would share his life story with me, considering my longtime interest in him, and looked forward to incorporating it with my own work. However, once he was dropped from Virgin Records he only worked on these memoirs sporadically for another couple of years, then shelved the project and settled into a constant state of touring and recording, with some of his recorded output released on his own label, Leon Russell Records. Leon continued with both of these activities right up until his 2016 death.

I kept Leon's text in my archives in case he ever resurrected the project. Then, in March, 2014, it looked like that was going to happen.

The call came on a Sunday afternoon. Leon and journalist Alanna Nash—whom he had met a few months earlier when she'd interviewed him for *Penthouse* magazine—happened to be at a Red Lobster in Mount Juliet, Tennessee. When he told me she was there with him, I immediately remembered a piece written by Alanna in the early 1970s that was one of the very first full-blown Leon Russell articles I'd ever read. I imparted this information to Leon, who chuckled and said, "Of course you know about her. I should have known."

Leon asked if I would send Alanna the Word Document files he'd forwarded to me all those years earlier, along with some pertinent photos from my Leon Russell archives, which I promptly did. Having written several biographies over the years, Alanna was no stranger to getting people's personal histories down on paper, and I was hopeful that she would be able to get Leon committed to doing a book about his life. She did work with him off and on for about a year, but Leon's constant touring made it difficult for the two to get together. A year or so later, the project simply died for lack of progress.

I had continued through the decades to research, write about, and lecture on Leon's contributions to our popular culture, with a special emphasis on his Hollywood session years, a period that had been of great interest to me ever since 1965, when I'd first become aware of his work. I had planned to publish everything in a book tentatively titled *Longhair Music*, but the amount of material, which included hundreds of recording sessions and photos, was becoming unmanageable.

Skip ahead to November 12, 2016 and a meeting between myself and my friend, writer John Wooley, whose books include biographies of the horror filmmaker Wes Craven and famed New York Yankees pitcher Ralph Terry, as well as a history of Oklahoma's music, *From the Blue Devils to Red Dirt*. On that particular day, John and I met in Tulsa to see if he would have an interest in collaborating on a Leon project. He was excited to join me. For more than 20 years, John had been an entertainment writer for the *Tulsa World*, where he'd chronicled not only Leon's career but scores of other members of the so-called Tulsa Sound. He knew the impact Leon had made not only on the Oklahoma music scene, but also nationally and internationally.

That day, John and I talked about the next steps to be taken to get *Longhair Music* into a manageable form, including a fresh interview or two with Leon himself. Then, at 6:41 the very next morning, I received a text from Leon's wife, Jan. It contained five simple but tragic words: *Leon died in his sleep.*

Sometime around 4:30 that morning Leon's mighty heart had given out, forever silencing one of the most renowned and talented individuals ever to hit the music industry—and eliminating forever the hope of an up-to-the-minute autobiography.

Remembering the 1992 text Leon had entrusted to me, I approached John about working on Leon's own memoirs first, and asked Jan for permission to make those 60 or so pages the basis of a book, complemented by photos from my archives. Because of the nature of Leon's reminiscences, John and I felt it would be necessary to occasionally provide some context for his words, so, when we thought it would make things clearer, we added our own annotations, as well as remembrances from people who knew him and worked with him. The latter were either taken from our files or, in several cases, acquired in brand-new interviews. Leon's own text was lightly edited for syntactical or, in a few cases, minor factual errors that could be attributed to simple slips of memory.

Which brings us to something else. In a couple of these chapters, he offers observations about co-workers and others that may seem harsh and unforgiving. His words in this book are a reflection of the way he felt when he wrote them, and as such are subject to the same tricks of remembering that bedevil us all. We know that Leon changed his mind about certain things—the recreational drug use celebrated in these pages, for instance. Despite his early fondness for alcohol while playing the clubs and, occasionally, during a recording session, as well as his eventual foray into the '60s and '70s hippie-drug scene, by the '80s he was shying away from all of that. This book ends with his leaving California, and we know that after he remarried and started a new life in Nashville, he put his family and livelihood first, promoting an anti-drug, anti-alcohol message around family members and friends until his death some 30 years later. John and I feel that he may well have changed his mind about some of the people he writes critically about in these pages, too.

While we know that Leon Russell fans worldwide—including us— would like to have had Leon's complete life story down for posterity, we're happy and honored to have been entrusted to share these glimpses into a special life. Leon may have come from humble beginnings, but because of his immense talent—along with, perhaps, fate and happenstance—he climbed to the very peak of the pop-music world.

This is the story of what happened while he was making that climb, and just afterwards. We hope you enjoy it.

—Steve Todoroff

Chapter One

IN THE BEGINNING

I HAVE ALWAYS EXPERIENCED severe stage fright, not only on stages, but in crowded rooms, lines for movies, and just about any place there's a lot of people who can be, by any stretch of the imagination, considered an audience. The psychologists call this agoraphobia: fear of the marketplace or fear of crowds.

In my case, I have to give credit for this paralyzing condition to one of my aunts on my father's side. At the age of four, I discovered my sex organs and, shortly thereafter, discovered that my female cousin had a completely different set. I was absolutely fascinated by this fact of nature and set out to do comprehensive research at my earliest opportunity. This occurred at a family gathering in Duncan, Oklahoma, where I found a secluded playhouse and immediately relieved my cousin of her panties. I was in the process of probing the situation in depth when who should arrive on the scene but my cousin's mother, in the form of my rather severe Aries aunt. She promptly paraded me in front of each individual adult family member and disclosed the nature of my research with scorching charges and descriptions.

That incident has affected me for my entire life. It has had an immeasurable detrimental effect on my career in show business in that I tend to freeze up around any situation that involves people watching me, even in an audition or interview. I've always harbored the suspicion that my audiences come to watch me deal with my secret phobia on stage.

Such is life.

The Bridges family in Apache, Oklahoma, July 1943. From left to right: Russell's mother, Hester; Russell; his father, John; and older brother Jerry (in front).

Russell's congenital condition, which involved his upper spine, was diagnosed as cerebral palsy a few months after this photo was taken. "We had no idea that Russell had anything wrong with him until that diagnosis," Hester told Steve Todoroff in 1987. "It somehow partially paralyzed his right side, particularly three fingers of his right hand. We did notice that once he started playing the piano it was good therapy for his right hand."

The affliction would play its part in shaping Russell's distinctive musical style.

Photo courtesy of Diane Sullivan. Courtesy of the Oklahoma Museum of Popular Culture/ Steve Todoroff Collection.

Claude Russell Bridges on April 2, 1946—his fourth birthday—in a photo taken at the family home in Apache, Oklahoma. Both his parents played piano, and it was around this time that Russell took an interest as well, without any prodding from either parent.

They were amazed, however, when he picked out the hymn "Trust and Obey" with his left hand, the one not affected by his birth injury, and then transposed it to his right. From that moment forward, the piano became a huge part of his life.

Photo courtesy of Diane Sullivan. Courtesy of the Oklahoma Museum of Popular Culture/Steve Todoroff Collection.

The Bridges men, circa 1944. Russell's paternal grandfather John Branson Bridges (second from left) stands next to sons Irvin (third from left) and Russell's father John (fourth from left), holding onto his son. Russell's brother, Jerry, is on the right. The other two youngsters are Irvin's boys Lloyd (left) and Irvin, Jr. (middle, next to Russell).

Photo courtesy of Brandon Bridges. Used with permission.

Chapter Two

TULSA NIGHTS

THERE WAS A thriving nightclub scene in Tulsa, Oklahoma when I was growing up. I didn't really appreciate it until I went to other cities and found music venues for young musicians to be almost nonexistent. I think the main factor was that Oklahoma was a "dry state" at the time, which meant you couldn't buy liquor—except at any nightclub or from bootleggers who would be happy to bring it to your door. Since there was no legal liquor, there was no legislation about operating hours for the clubs or any other cumbersome inconveniences.

I started working the "joints" at the age of fourteen. Piano players were hard to come by for some reason.

■■ ■■■

By the time I was in the seventh or eighth grade, the [Tulsa] guys who were graduating—in '58 or '59—had formed bands. You had Jumpin' Jack Dunham, and Tommy Rush and the Ambassadors, and the Swingin' Shadows. But there was a shortage of keyboard players. At that time, there just weren't a lot of guys taking piano lessons.

The guy I tried to emulate when I was in the seventh or eighth grade was Russell Bridges. We'd sneak into the Blue Moon, and I'd watch Leon play. He didn't know me from sic 'em, but I'd just sit at the side of the stage when we could sneak around and get into back doors and so on, or say we were with the band because we knew somebody.

At that time, from north, south, east, and west Tulsa, from Webster to Washington High School, to the new Edison, Central and Rogers, there were about 35 or 40 alleged bands trying to form. Everybody was trying to play rock 'n' roll. But the problem was, there were probably only about six piano players. I can remember every one of 'em.

—piano player Jim Blazer, *from a December 2003 interview with John Wooley*

Leon was just a skinny kid. He had gray hair. He wasn't old enough to have gray hair, but he did. Piano players weren't miking pianos, but he did, and he could make adjustments on the amp to give it a really unique sound. He used to play on an old upright piano at the Casa Del, and the Tropicana, and some of the other clubs we played.

—drummer Chuck Farmer, *from a December 2003 interview with John Wooley*

Leon sort of singlehandedly put the keyboard into the picture, You never could hear the piano in any [Tulsa] rock band. They didn't have amplification then. But through his persistence and his talent, he made it a big part of the sound.

—bassist Gerald Goodwin, *from a December 2003 interview with John Wooley*

■■ ■■■

When I was in high school, I worked a beer-joint job from six till eleven and then a private club from midnight to five a.m. I barely had time to sober up for school at nine a.m. and many times I would fall asleep with a terrible hangover in class. One club I played quite a lot paid ten dollars a night and all you could drink, and I drank all of it. By the time I finished high school, I was drinking at least a pint of hard liquor a day. There was not much talk of alcoholism at the time, even in the adult population.

Man, I can remember: We'd finish the gig, and we'd be sitting at the bar after hours, you know, drinking our gin. And Russell'd say, "Manry, why don't we just sit here and drink until we are gonna pass out, and then you come over to my house? I've got these extra bedrooms and everything, man, we'll go over there and pass out and get up in the morning and exchange licks."

I mean, to think you'd even have the energy to do such a thing. But this sounded completely normal to me, right? This was the way of life, you know. During those days, it was like another world. It was kind of like a Rat Pack situation. Russell and me hanging out at all the nightspots, and after hours. Oh, my God, it was incredible. I had no worries back then.

—piano player Jimmy Manry, *from a December 2003 interview with John Wooley*

■■　■■■

You can imagine my surprise when I arrived in California at the age of 17 and found that I had to be 21 to work in a nightclub. I had been working in clubs in Tulsa for three years and couldn't believe that even the musicians had to be 21 on the West Coast.

At the beginning of another trip to California, I stopped by the nightclub I've mentioned to see if the owner had anything I could take to keep me awake for the trip. He said, "Now, Russell, there's one thing I won't stand for around here, and that's dope-taking. It's not good for you and I won't have any of it." At which point he reached into his pocket and retrieved about 100 white-cross Benzedrine tablets, asking, "How many do you want?"

A very colorful and humorous figure from the gray realm between the underworld and respectability, he was, I suppose, the role model responsible for my somewhat hoodlum demeanor.

Another club I played all the time exploded one night, quite unexpectedly and completely. One minute it was there and the next minute it covered about three square blocks. This precipitated a series of bombings and fires that surely set a record of some kind in the annals of American nightclub history. After that initial explosion, there were six bombings and five fires in a ten-week period. Each and every club owner was convinced that his club was destroyed by his neighbor down the street to eliminate competition. It got so hairy that the FBI was called in to investigate, but no perpetrator of any of these events was ever found.

It was many years later, when I was playing Bill Graham's Fillmore East in New York, that another bandleader came backstage to see me. We started talking about the "good old days" back in Tulsa, and that first club explosion, and he said, "Yeah, I worked at that fucking joint. They wouldn't pay me, so I put thirty-five sticks of dynamite in there and blew up their fucking joint!" He went on to tell me how he had put five sticks behind the bar, six on the stage, three behind the jukebox, etc. It was pretty close to the FBI estimate of the amount of explosives used for the job.

I hesitate to reveal the name of the famous Arkansas rocker; there is always the possibility he might decide to blow up my fucking joint.

There's no business like show business.

There was a club on Greenwood Avenue in Tulsa called the Flamingo. It was the local version of many black music halls that proliferated throughout America before all of the commotion about civil rights. In those days, the ghetto was invisible and nonexistent to the white power structure. The philosophy was, "If they stay on their side of town, they can do anything they want," and that is just exactly what "they" did.

At the Flamingo, my contemporaries and I, at the ages of about 15 or 16, were treated to full revues that lasted until five or six in the morning and happened every night of the week. I never once saw a policeman when I was there and liquor by the drink, gambling of various types, and prostitution were the order of the day.

But mainly, there was the music. It was not uncommon to see a twenty-piece house band, with perhaps as many as ten featured entertainers, in a period from 11 p.m. to five a.m. The place was a goldmine of influence for a young musician, who might be able to see Billy Eckstine, Dinah Washington, and Big Joe Turner in the same week. I first saw Clifford Scott, the fantastic saxophone player with

Bill Doggett on the record "Honky Tonk," there. A nearby place on Apache called the Big Ten Ballroom was where I saw Bobby Bland with Junior Parker, Ray Charles, and, with a larger-than-capacity crowd, Jackie Wilson.

Certainly, far and away the most colorful entertainer I saw in that period of time was Esquerita. He made Little Richard look like a choirboy; in fact, I have heard it said that Richard got a lot of his outrageousness from Esquerita. I can well believe it. Esquerita's standard wardrobe consisted of toreador pants that looked as though they were painted on and a see-through blouse covered with sequins, along with high-heeled pumps, jewelry, mascara, and false eyelashes that would make even Tammy Faye Bakker blush.

He came up to me one night and said, "Honey, come up to my room at the Small Hotel, and if I can't make you scream in 30 seconds, I'll give you my color TV and stereo." That was his main priority, trying to give away that TV and stereo.

Once, he was arrested for causing a five-car accident on Tulsa's 21st Street, merely by standing beside the road.

Scream it, honey!

∎∎ ∎∎∎

Editors' note: Born in Greenville, South Carolina as Eskew Reeder Jr., Esquerita was indeed an inspiration for young Richard Penniman. In The Life and Times of Little Richard *by Charles White (Harmony Books, 1984), Richard talks about meeting Esquerita in a Macon, Georgia bus station in the early 1950s. The two went to Richard's house, where Esquerita played "One Mint Julep" on the piano, "way up in the treble," with a "fantastic" bass line:*

"I said, 'Hey, how do you do that?' And he says, 'I'll teach you.' And that's when I really started playing.' . . . He was—still is—one of the greatest pianists and that's including Jerry Lee Lewis, Stevie Wonder, or anybody I've ever heard. I learned a whole lot about phrasing from him. He really taught me a lot."

Esquerita died in 1988 at the age of 50.

Tulsa's Flamingo Club, seen here in a rare photograph from the late 1930s, was the "goldmine of influence" where a teenaged Russell and his music-loving contemporaries regularly ventured to watch marathon stage revues featuring the top African-American performers of the day. In those segregated times, the "black part of town," exemplified by Greenwood Avenue—where the Flamingo Club and other live-music establishments were located—offered nightly escapes into a world overflowing with thrills and wonder.

Photo courtesy J. Kavin Ross/Greenwood Tribune. Used with permission.

During his teenage years, Russell also frequented the city's bigger showplaces. At the Municipal Theatre in downtown Tulsa, for instance, he took in shows from rock 'n' roll stars Jerry Lee Lewis (with whom he would soon tour), Chuck Berry, Little Richard, and Clyde McPhatter, as well as a concert by the famed classical violinist Jascha Heifetz. Later, when he was headlining his own national tours as Leon Russell, he would perform many times in the same venue, which was renamed the Brady Theatre in the 1970s. The annual Leon Russell Birthday Bash was held at the Brady from 1986 through 2013.

Photo by Steve Todoroff. Courtesy of the Oklahoma Museum of Popular Culture/ Steve Todoroff Collection.

Chapter Three

JERRY LEE

Around 1960 we went out with Jerry Lee Lewis and played places in Kansas, Nebraska, and Wyoming, and some had chicken wire in front of the stage to keep people from throwing things, beer bottles and such, at the band.

—drummer Chuck Blackwell, *from a June 20, 1987 interview with Steve Todoroff*

■■ ■■■

WHEN I FIRST met Jerry Lee Lewis [in 1959], he had just married his cousin and been run out of England for his trouble. He was down in spirit and finances and was attempting to tour the U.S. without a band and for very little money. It was during this time that my group was hired to back him for his appearance at Tulsa's Cain's Ballroom, the home of Bob and Johnnie Lee Wills and the regular house band at the time, Benny Ketchum and His Western Playboys, from Bartlesville. Cain's is a giant warehouse-type dancehall from the '30s, long and narrow, the walls lined with pictures of a virtual *Who's Who* in country music.

Wonder of wonders—my band was going to get to play with "The Killer." Of course, I wouldn't personally get to play while Jerry Lee was on stage, since we both played piano, but I would get to enjoy watching him start the show—with no rehearsal—and realize about halfway into the second song that he wasn't going to be able to play anything the band didn't know. Since we *had* rehearsed and discussed the arrangements of all his records, our group members were even able to play the songs in the style of his regular band, which was Russell Smith on drums and J.W. Brown on bass. (Brown, incidentally, was the father of the cousin who caused Jerry Lee's untimely departure from Great Britain.) They even knew how to play the ones that he hadn't played before. I had spent a good deal of time discussing with them methods of playing songs you didn't know.

After that show, Jerry Lee admitted he had been having a terrible time playing with pickup bands and, even though he didn't know how, he had to have us on the road with him. Well, the way he did it was that he didn't pay us very much. But we didn't care. We would have gone for nothing. I changed the oil in my '51 Chrysler Imperial limousine and we were off on the great adventure—show business on the road!

II III

Editors' note: Posters for these Jerry Lee Lewis tours list "Johnny Williams and the Hollywood Starlighters" as an added attraction, often with the line "featuring Russell Bridges." Even though they weren't even out of their teens, saxophonist Williams and the Starlighters, with Leon on piano, were already an established Tulsa act by the time they went on tour with Lewis, as Williams explained to John Wooley in an interview conducted February 26, 2018:

In 1958, '59, during the school year, we worked at Griff's Supper Club in Tulsa, at Admiral and Pittsburgh, across the street from a graveyard. I was kind of a hustler, you know, and got to asking questions, and I was a pretty good salesman, so I wound up booking the band, making the arrangements.

We were making $60 a week playing five nights a week at Griff's Supper Club, playing mostly standards. At that time, Earl Bostic and [Bill] Doggett were big, so we played quite a few of their tunes, too. I remember Russell said, "I get so tired of backing that saxophone up. That's all they want to hear."

But he knew a lot of standard tunes. He taught me every standard tune I knew. And I really had to listen, because if I didn't play it right he'd plink the right note [on the piano] and I'd say, "Russell, don't do that."

He'd say, "Listen."

It was a partnership, really and truly, between all of us. Me and Russell were kind of the head of the chain.

The original five [members] were me, Chuck Blackwell, Russell, [bassist] Lucky Clark, and [guitarist] Leo Feathers. We got the name Starlighters when we were still in high school, getting ready to play some school dances and so forth. I was going with a girl named Linda Parsons, and we were out at her house, on Apache [Street] by the airport, practicing for this dance. And her mother, Sue Parsons, who was helping us make a poster, said, "You guys need to come up with a name.*"*

She mentioned the name the Starlighters. Well, everybody liked that okay, and of course with me being her girl's boyfriend, she said, "Let's make it Johnny Williams and the Starlighters." So that's how that came about. To tell you the truth, I don't know how they enhanced that to the Hollywood Starlighters [for the Lewis shows]. I have no idea.

We backed up a lot of the different singers and artists that came to town. I guess we were the band of choice to back 'em up. We worked with Frogman Henry and Little Richard, just a whole bunch of different ones who'd come into town and need a band. The first time we ever backed up Lewis, at Cain's Ballroom, Lewis came up on the stand and he said, "I'm not playing that piano. He plays 'way better than I do." When we'd do some kind of a hop or something, for kids, Russell would do Lewis stuff, and I guess we knew all of his tunes as well as he did. So Lewis didn't play the piano hardly at all, maybe one or two songs, that night. He stood up and sang the tunes and Russell played the piano.

It seems like we did four or five tours [with Lewis], and they'd last for maybe 20-30 days. It was over the whole summer of '59 we did that, and maybe just a little bit before. I don't think we had over a total of three or four months of tours with him. Part of the time, we were his backup band, and then part of the time we were the opening act. Probably fifty percent of the tours, he had J.W. Brown and a little skinny drummer [Editors' note: This is probably Russell Smith] with him, and they did a three-piece Jerry Lee Lewis act. We would open for them. When Lewis found out we could back him up, I guess he thought, "I don't need you guys," and left 'em at home.

I was our business manager, and every week we'd get a paycheck. It wasn't that much money, but Lewis's booking agent wrote me several hot checks, and I'd have to get after him and threaten him and this and that. They had JP [Justices of the Peace] courts back then, and they were pretty efficient. One time when he owed us money he was down in Woodward, Oklahoma and I filed charges with the JP there. They picked his rear up and were getting ready to put him in jail, but he came up with the money.

■■ ■■■

I didn't trust anybody else's driving, since I was 16 and an expert in my own right, so I drove after the shows until one or two in the afternoon, let the band go set up while I went to the motel to sleep, then showed up to play the opening portion of the show, usually at about eight o'clock.

The face of the American countryside was considerably different then, without the Holiday Inns, the Interstates, and the truck stops. Many nights we would be 100 miles, in every direction, away from an open gas station or restaurant. Sometimes, we would have to sleep in the car for six or seven hours parked outside a gas station, waiting for them to open because we were out of gas. It's funny how easily we take things for granted today, like being able to find fuel stops and hotels when they're needed.

■■ ■■■

I remember this one place in Cheyenne, Wyoming turned into a complete riot. It was unbelievable. People just fighting and crashing and breaking bottles across the bar. It looked like something out of the movies. Then they turned on the band and started throwing things at us.

Jerry Lee split first and left us playing, but the head bouncer covered us and we got out okay.

—Chuck Blackwell, *from the June 27, 1987 Todoroff interview*

We played Cheyenne, Wyoming in the dead of winter. During the show, a riot broke out and three to four hundred people spent the last half of the show battling it out as Jerry Lee stood on the piano bench and sang and watched. I'll never forget the image of the Killer leaving the stage entrance with gun in hand, in the style of a Brink's guard, walking to his Caddy for another show in another town.

As we were on our way to the next show, we were obliged to go through a mountain pass on a two-lane road that was narrow and steep, our old limousine and U-Haul making a valiant effort to overcome the grade. I first had a hint we were in trouble when I noticed the speedometer was still reading 40 miles per hour even as we were slowing to a stop. I thought at first that the transmission was failing, but when the speedometer reading remained the same and we started traveling backwards, I realized we had trouble of a different variety. The road was icy, with no guardrails, and shoulders that descended into the blackness of a Hell that piqued the horror of the imagination. I finally took my foot off the gas and, after about ten seconds, we stopped sliding backwards.

The first plan was to unhook the trailer, turn the car around, and go back down the road to get a better run at the incline and perhaps a bit more momentum. Even though the road was so slick it was difficult to stand up, we got the trailer unhooked and turned around. Then, with the driver's door open so I could jump out (if events took a nasty turn), I managed to finally get the car headed in the opposite direction.

When we got to the bottom of the hill, we repeated the whole process once again. Only this time we didn't get as far as our first attempt before sliding dangerously near the edge of the road to a stop. Sitting there for about three hours, we watched four-wheel-drive vehicles and Volkswagens pass us by until we were finally pulled over the crest of the mountain by a helpful gasoline-truck driver.

Ah, the unfathomable vistas of a life in art.

We were in Kiowa, Kansas, in this hall with this old stage, you know, and the place was packed. Jerry Lee Lewis had appendicitis, and he was afraid that the people were going to riot. So they had the local doctor come up and tell everybody that they could have their money back, or they could stay if they wanted.

Well, it was worth their while, because Leon got up and did Jerry Lee Lewis. He kicked the piano bench back. The dust flew from this old stage. And he jumped up on this and that and, yeah, I'd never seen him put on a show like that.

They got their money's worth. I guess when the show was on him, he got with it. Of course, later on he proved he was always up to the task.

—Chuck Blackwell, *from a December 2003 interview with John Wooley*

■■ ■■■

Lewis was easy to work with, but he was a wino. In Kansas, we was doing a show, and he got to drinking all this rotgut, or wine, or whatever he was drinking, and Russell went out and did his [Lewis's] show. We thought the crowd was gonna lynch us, but Russell went out there and did the whole show and kicked the piano stool back and the whole deal, and nobody wanted their money back.

He was supposed to have had appendicitis. But we didn't know if it was appendicitis or rotgut.

—Johnny Williams, *from the February 26, 2018 Wooley interview*

■■ ■■■

Also with us on the Jerry Lee Lewis tour was [rockabilly act] Bobby Lee Trammell of Jonesboro, Arkansas, who could teach a trick or two to modern new-wave and punk entertainers. In fact, he may have personally invented the maneuver in which the performer jumps ten feet off a stage into the middle of the audience, with no concern for personal injury or the well-being of the spectators. The man would literally do anything. One time in L.A. he climbed to the top of the transmission tower for radio station KWFB and threatened to jump if they didn't play his new record within a certain amount of time.

Needless to say, they played his record and he received a substantial amount of press through the wire services around the world.

Later, Bobby Lee took over the recording division of "Dare to be Great" motivational speaker Glenn W. Turner's business. Mr. Turner was subsequently prosecuted in a pyramid-sales fraud scandal by the Securities and Exchange Commission.

It's only rock 'n' roll but I like it.

Editors' note: According to the August 21, 1987 New York Times, Glenn Turner and his business partner Edward G. Rechtor were both sentenced to seven years in prison "for using an illegal pyramid scheme to bilk people out of thousands of dollars." The two had been convicted in July of 19 counts of conspiracy, fraud, and promoting a pyramid scheme.

Johnny Williams and the Starlighters, seen here in a shot at Tulsa's Tropicana Club, circa 1959—the year they went on tour with Jerry Lee Lewis. From left to right: guitarist Leo Feathers, drummer Chuck Blackwell, bassist Rick Ryles (sitting in for regular band member Lucky Clark), saxophonist Williams, and pianist Russell Bridges.

Photo by Jimmy Markham. Courtesy of the Oklahoma Museum of Popular Culture/ Steve Todoroff Collection.

No Shakes For Jerry Lee

KIOWA — There wasn't "A Whole Lot of Shakin' Going On" by rock and roller Jerry Lee Lewis at the dance in Veterans Memorial building Thursday night. Jerry Lee was having his appendix removed at Kiowa Hospital.

The entertainer was reported in good condition Friday, following his appendectomy, and members of his family were on their way from Ferriday, La., to be with him.

The dance went on as scheduled, with Jerry Lee's bass player and drummer joining with the Hollywood Starliners — from Tulsa, Okla. — to provide music. The Starliners had been scheduled to appear with the rock and roll star.

Johnny Edwards, the Lewis group's chauffeur, said they would miss a Friday night date at Wichita Falls, Tex., and a later one near there, but planned to be able to appear in Hollywood Nov. 19 as scheduled.

The poster for the infamous Kiowa, Kansas gig, in which Russell had to take over for incapacitated headliner Jerry Lee Lewis. Note the "featuring Russell Bridges" notation at bottom right.

Photo courtesy of the Oklahoma Museum of Popular Culture/Steve Todoroff Collection.

Appendicitis or rotgut? According to this clipping from the November 7, 1959 edition of the *Hutchinson* (Kansas) *News*, Lewis indeed had a bad appendix that needed to be removed. Because of his surgery and recovery, dates in Wichita Falls, Texas (on November 6) and Vernon, Texas (November 7) had to be canceled. So the tour essentially ended at this point, after about two months of road work, and Johnny Williams, Russell, and the rest of the Starlighters headed back home.

Photo courtesy of The Hutchinson News. Used with permission.

Chapter Four

THE ACCENTS

I'**VE BEEN THINKING** about an old bass player from high school who's a lawyer now. He stopped by to see me in Houston the other day with Joe Welling, another high-school acquaintance.

■■ ■■■

[Editors' note: Joe Welling was the leader of Little Joe and the Strangers, an early Tulsa rock 'n' roll group, as well as Leon's fellow Will Rogers High School student.]

■■ ■■■

I am reminded of the time this bassist went to the club in California where J.J. Cale, Chuck Blackwell, and he and I were working. He picked up the paycheck for the entire band, took it to Las Vegas, and gambled it all away, having to walk the last five miles because the new Buick Rivera convertible his daddy had bought for him had run out of gas. That's what he told us, anyway. I always suspected that the Buick was really only a block away and that he told the story to garner a little sympathy from his victims, who otherwise would not necessarily have been so disposed. It *sounds* like a lawyer trick.

He and I originally went to California with David Gates, another old high-school band member. We had a band called the Accents that played numerous high-school dances and other functions.

David was my first indication that the entire population might not be influenced by the Golden Rule. Our little band sort of came to an untimely end when a big record company in New York flew David in and convinced him—without much effort, I suspect—that he would be better off dropping us in favor of New York studio musicians. I believe the A&R representative in that instance was Tony Alamo, who later received much acclaim as a religious leader and child abuser.

■■ ■■■

Editors' notes: Traditionally, the A&R (Artist & Repertoire) person at a record label has been responsible for finding musical acts and supervising their recording, which usually includes suggestions on what to record and with whom to record it.

Born Bernie Lazar Hoffman in 1934, Joplin, Missouri native Tony Alamo was the evangelist-founder of the Arkansas-based Alamo Christian Foundation (now Tony Alamo Christian Ministries). In 2009, he was convicted of sexually abusing young girls and sent to prison. Alamo's ministry, often referred to as a cult, grew out of his involvement in the Hollywood-based "Jesus Freak" movement of the late 1960s.

Not to be confused with the 1940s and '50s vocalist Tony Alamo, best known for his work with big-band leader Sammy Kaye, this Tony Alamo may well have been the A&R man for the David Gates record. Writing for the allmusic.com *site, Alex Henderson identified him as someone who "worked in the music industry as a manager/record promoter in the '50s and early '60s." However, as Guy Lancaster wrote in the* Encyclopedia of Arkansas History and Culture *(www.encyclopediaofarkansas.net), "Much of the information on Alamo's early, pre-conversion life is spurious at best, on account of Alamo's constant exaggerations of his importance and/or sinfulness."*

After Alamo moved to the West Coast in the '60s, added Lancaster, "He apparently adopted the name Marcus Abad for some time and achieved some modicum of success as a 'big band crooner' in Los Angeles, California. Alamo went on to own a health club and work in the music industry. He claimed that he recorded a hit record single in the early 1960s, 'Little

Yankee Girl,' and that he was asked to manage musical acts including the Beatles, the Doors, and the Rolling Stones."

("Little Yankee Girl," was released in 1964 on the Little Mark label as by Marcus Abad but failed to chart nationally.)

Alamo died in prison in 2017.

☷ ☷☷

David also introduced me to scuba diving. I had never been before, so he gave me a unit with a hole in the hose, thinking it would be a good laugh. I will never forget that feeling of the water rushing into my lungs as I was in a state of dangerous disorientation, not being able to find the surface of the water. It was very funny indeed.

After we'd moved out to California, I got a call one day from a friend of mine named Kim Fowley. He was looking for songs for a new girl group he was producing. I asked David if he would like to play some of our songs for him, and he said, 'I don't want to have anything to do with that guy." So I ended up playing some of the demos we'd done for him, and he had a top-ten record with one of the songs that David wrote, "Popsicles and Icicles," recorded by a female trio called the Murmaids.

☷ ☷☷

Editors' note: Another infamous figure from 1960s Hollywood, Kim Fowley was a wildly colorful music promoter, publisher, producer, and occasional performer. "Popsicles and Icicles," released in 1963, was one of several '60s hits he was involved with, the most famous being The Hollywood Argyles' 1960 record "Alley Oop," which he co-produced. Fowley is perhaps best-known for his management of the '70s girl group the Runaways.

Fowley died of bladder cancer in 2015.

☷ ☷☷

When David and I were dissolving our fledgling publishing association for the last time, we signed a contract listing all the copyrights we owned together. They included "Popsicles and Icicles," but David admitted that I didn't really own half of the song because he had "removed" my copy of the contract and I couldn't possibly prove my co-ownership. Just an all-around funny guy.

David was, in fact, a very accomplished songwriter and later enjoyed much success with his group Bread—whose first album cover featured many pictures of money in various denominations—and later as a solo artist.

The first-ever publicity photo of David Gates and the Accents, circa 1957. From left to right: Gates, drummer Don Kimmel, bassist Gerald Goodwin, and pianist Russell Bridges. This group became one of the top rock 'n' roll bands in Oklahoma, playing numerous high school dances, private parties, and college fraternity and sorority events as well as releasing two regional singles.

After the original group broke up, Gates would re-use the Accents name many times over the years—when he and Russell began working together in Southern California, for instance, and again to label an all-Tulsa trio consisting of himself, Russell, and drummer Chuck Blackwell. In the early '60s, that band appeared onstage in Van Nuys, California in an all-star event dubbed the Valley Teenage Spectacular Show. Sponsored by the Van Nuys Junior Chamber of Commerce, the concert included appearances by Johnny Burnette, Jerry Wallace, Dick and Dee Dee, the Casteels, and Jan & Dean.

Photo courtesy of the Oklahoma Museum of Popular Culture/Steve Todoroff Collection.

Chapter Five

CALIFORNIA DREAMIN'

I still had two years of high school to go when they [Leon and Chuck Blackwell] split to California. I didn't get a chance to even go until 1961, when I got out of high school. He had already been out here I don't know how many times.

—drummer Jim Karstein, *from a September 9, 1982 interview with Diane Sullivan*

■■ ■■■

IT'S AMAZING THAT I didn't in up in jail, or dead, or both after I arrived in California for the first time. Except for the Jerry Lee Lewis tour, I had never been away from home for any length of time and was completely inexperienced and naïve about the ways of the real world.

When I finally arrived in California, the job that I had been promised lasted exactly one night. After that time I didn't work for about six months, freeloading off whomever I could to survive. Once, when I was staying at the apartment of a person from Oklahoma I barely knew, I decided that since I was in the Golden State I really should take a trip to the beach.

It was not a wise move, considering I hadn't been in the sun for more than five or ten minutes at a stretch in my entire lifetime.

My landlord/acquaintance took me out to a rather deserted section of beach about 10 in the morning and came back for me at six. By that time I was almost in shock. For the next three months, I pulled two- and three-foot sections of skin off my body. The pain was intense.

About that same time, this landlord/acquaintance robbed a gas station while I was sitting in his car and the attendant was busy with the pump.

All things considered, I guess I was pretty lucky. I could've easily ended up a cast member on [the horror TV series] *Tales from the Darkside.*

II III

Editors' note: In addition to playing clubs, much of Leon's early work in California involved playing on demos for the music-publishing outfit Metric Music. Generally speaking, demos were not commercial recordings, made instead to demonstrate (hence the name) the merits of a particular song, in the hopes that a recording artist would pick it up and cut it. Although doing demo work could be lucrative, it didn't pay as well as doing sessions for commercial recordings. Leon soon graduated to that sort of session work.

He quit taking the demos, the more legit sessions he got. That's the whole process. You start out doing demos, and if you're any good the big guys will call you. You move on up. Well, Leon was good enough that he started getting the "uptown" sessions. . . .

Leon got in with Ricky Nelson, Joe Osborn [Nelson's bassist], and James Burton [Nelson's guitarist]. He started playing with them [and] [h]e got to know some of those session players because Ricky was on TV, and James Burton and Joe Osborn really liked Leon . . . . [E]very time you did a session, if you did good, *everybody wanted to use you.*

—singer-songwriter-guitarist JJ Cale, *from a September 9, 1982 interview with Diane Sullivan*

When Leon started getting in with those people he worked his way in through the nightclub scene, and at that time everybody was down in Downey and Norwalk. . . . Guys would come in and there were really some good jam sessions going on over the weekends. Leon started meeting

Joe Osborn, James Burton, and Tommy Allsup through the nightclub scene.

Like I said, when I came out in 1961 he had already been out here [in California] at least twice, maybe three times. When I first came out here, just about that time, he started into the sessions. By mid-1962, he was the hottest player in town. Once he got in there, it didn't take him long to go right to the top of the stack.

—Jim Karstein, *from the September 9, 1982 Sullivan interview*

II III

On December 7, 1961, I played my first "real" session with the "main guys." It happened in Liberty Studios, where I'd been working almost every day on demos for Metric Music, which was a publishing subsidiary of Liberty Records. Many nights I had stood outside one studio or another and watched people like Earl Palmer, who would arrive in his new Cadillac. Now, here I was on the "inside," with Earl playing drums and Barney Kessel on guitar.

I could barely contain my excitement at the prospect of playing with these great musicians. The arranger was Ernie Freeman. The first session I played for him was with Johnny Burnette; I did many with Ernie Freeman after that.

In those days, I did quite a lot of work with Gary Paxton. Those days came well before his resurgence as a religious recording artist, and he was drinking a lot of whiskey then, as well as taking the odd Benzedrine tablet. He was known for hiring the down-and-out and was a big supporter of musicians in general, cutting records on them as well as giving them paying work playing on his productions. The first Paxton session I played on was for Bobby "Boris" Pickett of "Monster Mash" fame, for the album that followed Pickett's hit single.

II III

There was always a bunch of us Oklahoma hillbillies out there [in California], but at this particular time it was mostly just Leon and me. I was living in a boarding house and he was up the road a mile or so, where he had an apartment. During that period, he was making his meteoric rise to the top of the session-musician pack, and he and I were hanging out a lot. . . . A lot of times he'd have to go into his first session at 9 a.m., and he might not get done until after midnight, so I'd run his errands for him, take him places and pick him up.

[One night] [t]he session was over when I walked in, and all the lights were down, except for a light on this lone microphone. The way it was lit, it was almost theatrical. It was late, it was dark, and they were doing an overdub, with two people at the microphone, blowing into these glasses, or paper cups—I can't remember exactly—with straws. The glasses, I remember, were two different sizes, so they could get two different sounds.

I didn't really know Bobby Pickett, and I don't even recall being introduced to him that night, but I'm guessing he was one of the people blowing into the straws. They were playing the song back and overdubbing those sounds. And of course when you hear that record and you hear that boiling, bubbling sound for the mad scientist's lab, that's what you're hearing. At the time, I thought, "Wow. Isn't that clever?"

—Jim Karstein, *from an August 2008 interview with John Wooley*

■■ ■■■

I also did sessions for Del-Fi, a label owned by a colorful character named Bob Keane, who was an ex-clarinet player turned entrepreneur. On one occasion, I played a Del-Fi session for a Bobby and Johnny Crawford record. I don't remember Bobby doing much more, but Johnny was on the TV show *The Rifleman* at the time and had a couple of hits as a recording artist.

■■ ■■■

Editors' note: The sessions Leon played on yielded the only single release from the Crawford Brothers, "Good Buddies" b/w "You Gotta Wear Shoes," released by Del-Fi in December of 1962. It did not chart. Earlier that year, Johnny had scored three top 20 hits for the label: "Cindy's Birthday," "Your Nose Is Gonna Grow," and "Rumors."

Like Johnny, Bobby Crawford was also featured in a television western at the time, having a recurring role as the younger brother of star John Smith's character, Slim Sherman, in the series Laramie. *He acted into the late '60s and then went into film production, producing such high-profile features as 1982's* The World According to Garp *and 1988's* Funny Farm.

■■ ■■■

For a time, I was the organ player for the Ventures, playing on "Telstar," "Red River Rock," and other songs. And during that period I played on quite a few records with Johnny Rivers before he found his niche at the Whisky a Go Go and cut his hit version of "Memphis."

I also played piano for Jackie DeShannon, who was a writer for Metric at the time, when she did a showcase at the Band Box on La Cienega Boulevard. [Music producer] Jack Nitzsche was in the audience. From that time forward, I played on almost every record he made.

Not far from the Band Box on La Cienega was an expensive barber shop—later made even more famous by the dark deeds of the Manson family—that I finally patronized upon the recommendation of many of my hair-conscious friends.

■■ ■■■

[Editors' note: Here, Leon is likely referring to the innovative hair stylist Jay Sebring, who was, along with actress Sharon Tate, a victim in the infamous Cielo Drive murders perpetrated by Charles Manson's disciples in 1969.]

■■ ■■■

I went to the shop with hair that looked vaguely like that of the Little Rascals' Alfalfa and came out looking, in my own estimation at least, like a movie star. I remember gazing at myself in the rear-view for all of half an hour, ecstatic that I was finally and forever divorced from the chronic rooster tail that had plagued me for my entire life.

In fact, I looked so good that I started wearing tailor-made outfits by Harvey Krantz, "Tailor for the Stars." It was the first time in my life that I'd had the least interest in clothes.

All was moving along swimmingly until one fateful day. I was running late for a Frank Sinatra session and didn't have time to go through the plastering-down ceremony with the magic pink hairspray that was merchandised at the magic barber shop on La Cienega. Also, as luck would have it, I was also overdue for my magic haircut and, accordingly, my somewhat less-than-magic hair was too long.

The result of these facts created a hairy situation indeed. The effect that was achieved was similar to the one attained by the Rolling Stones in later times, but at that time it was not even imagined in the wildest Pentecostal nightmare.

There I was, rushing into the session at the last minute in my fastidiously matched Harvey Krantz ensemble, with my normally perfect movie-star hair hanging almost to my shoulders. The abuse that was consequently heaped on me by my contemporaries was immediate and overwhelming. People I worked with every day, whom I considered to be my friends, couldn't get in my face quickly enough to tell me, with great vehemence, what an idiot I looked like and that I should be ashamed of myself for going out in public in such a fashion.

Primarily concerned with being late, I had forgotten about the hair situation, so it wasn't until about the third attack that I realized they were expressing their displeasure about my coif! Frank himself honored me with an icy stare that resulted in a minor collision between Mr. S. and unfortunately placed post in his path. I wondered if that might end up being my major contribution to pop music.

At any rate, I learned a very important lesson that day about prejudice and the absolute hatred that people are capable of expressing toward others they perceive to be different and perhaps not quite as good as themselves. I decided right then and there that no matter how uncomfortable or inconvenient it might be, I was never going to cut my hair again. I didn't want to forget this particularly nasty component of human nature, realizing also that people would only be too happy to display it for me if I followed this conviction. Later, I was to find on many occasions that I was grouped with my brothers of darker pigmentation when it came to being refused service in restaurants and access to rest-room facilities after purchasing fuel at gas stations. In Denver, Colorado one time I played a concert before an audience of 10,000 and the next day was refused service at a Mr. Steak on Colfax Avenue in that same city.

It all gave me a rare look into the rampant prejudice of my country and in my entire species. The world looked the same to me, with or without magic hair, but once I let it go the world seemed to view me from an entirely different perspective.

Curiouser and curiouser.

I had the chance to play on many Phil Spector records at Gold Star Studios on Santa Monica Boulevard. The studio he worked in was designed to hold about five musicians, six at the most; Phil managed to get in 25, with almost enough room left over for someone to walk.

The first time I heard the band play in that small room was truly inspirational. Phil's normal lineup was one or two drummers, two percussionists, five guitarists, electric and acoustic bass players, five or six horn players, three or four pianists, and the present mayor of Palm Springs *[Sonny Bono, Palm Springs' mayor from April 1988 through April 1992]* on tambourine. It was truly overpowering. Jack Nitzsche was the arranger, and because I had started doing most of Jack's piano work, I got on the Spector sessions.

On the first one I attended, Phil came up to me and made some sort of hand sign, as if he might be warding off a vampire, and said, "Dumb. Play dumb." He was very fond of the idea that the audience for pop music was incapable of digesting anything burdened with too much content.

It was interesting at first. But most of the sessions ran seven to eight hours, with the same mundane figures played again and again, except for minor changes or attempted improvements. One day in particular it was starting to *drive me crazy!* Unfortunately, I followed the lead of my friend and copyist, Roy Caton, who was playing trumpet on the session, and went next door to the liquor store, where I bought a pint of peach-flavored vodka.

It was a mistake.

About two or three hours and 80 takes later, I was standing on top of the Steinway, doing a pretty good impression of A.A. Allen *[one of Leon's favorite televangelists—see Chapter Nine]*. That's about all I remember, except for an exchange with Phillip, which started when he said through the talkback mike, "Leon, don't you know what teamwork means?"

"Phil, do you know what '*fuck you*' means?" I returned.

It was all innocent fun, but Phil's mother was there and his body-guards were there, and right about when they were getting ready to break my neck, he held them off and said I was usually a good guy.

The next day, I didn't recall too much about the whole incident, but Tommy Tedesco, a jovial, Mafioso-type guitar-player friend of mine who'd played on the session, came over to my apartment and offered to finance a religious tour for me in exchange for half the profits. "I'm serious about this, now, Leon; I'm not kidding. I'll put up the money for a big tent and trucks and whatever we need. We'll make millions," he told me, a pronounced financial gleam in his eye. I actually thought he was putting me on, but he referred to his offer many times over the next few months.

Phil Spector had a comedic style similar to Don Rickles, using it in his sessions to get a few laughs at the expense of the players—most often Tedesco or [drummer] Hal Blaine. It was humorous enough, under the circumstances. But then, years later in England, I was with many of the British stars—including Eric Clapton, George Harrison, and Gary Wright—who had turned out for a session with Phil's wife, Veronica. When he tried that sort of humor, the musicians just sort of looked at one another with dismay.

Different times, different lines.

Here, Russell plays one of three keyboards (with Al DeLory to his left and Don Randi to his right) on a session for producer Phil Spector at L.A.'s Gold Star Studios. Using multiples of several different instruments was a key part of Spector's trademark "Wall of Sound."

Photo by Ray Avery. Used with permission.

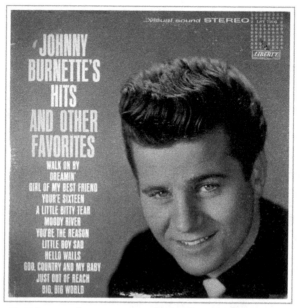

On December 7, 1961, according to American Federation of Musicians archives, Russell played on his first legitimate union recording session. Under the direction of well-known keyboardist, arranger, and producer Ernie Freeman, it was held at the Liberty Records studio for singer Johnny Burnette, whose recent hits for the label included "You're Sixteen" and "God, Country And My Baby." At the time, Freeman and Liberty producer Snuff Garrett were attempting to put the country-music-influenced vocalist into more of a pop-music mode. (Songs from this session were released on the 1962 LP pictured here.)

Also on the session was guitarist Tommy Allsup, a northeastern Oklahoma native who'd not only helped a newly arrived Russell find work in California clubs but also had hired him to work on the non-union demo recordings that ultimately eased Russell into session jobs. Other players on that December 7 date included still another Oklahoman, guitarist Barney Kessel, a session veteran, drummer Earl Palmer, and bassist Red Callender.

Although the AFM required members to be 21 years old to play union sessions, Russell was four months shy of turning 20 when he made his official debut. Legend has it that he had a fake ID on file with Tulsa Local 94, so when the L.A. branch of the union checked with its Tulsa counterpart, Russell's hometown office confirmed the untruth that he was indeed 21.

Courtesy of the Oklahoma Museum of Popular Culture/Steve Todoroff Collection.

This photo of, from left, Russell, Ricky Nelson, an unidentified man, and producer-arranger Jimmy Haskell hung in Russell's Skyhill Drive home in California for many years. Russell had been introduced to Nelson, who was then a bona fide teenage heartthrob and recording and television star, by Nelson's guitarist James Burton, one of the players Russell had become acquainted with through after-hours jam sessions in the Norwalk-Downey area. At the time he met Burton, as well as other Nelson band members, Russell was still scuffling to get established, and Burton's friendship and help proved especially invaluable.

Nelson, impressed by Russell's talent, soon began using him in live shows. Russell went on to play, and sing the occasional backup vocal, on many of Nelson's Decca recording sessions.

Courtesy of Kelly Poorboy. Used with permission.

Chapter Six

SMALL SCREEN/BIG SCREEN

FOR A WHILE, I was working on an ABC-TV show called *Shindig*, created by Jack Good. It was the Americanized version of an English effort called *Ready Steady Go!*

■■ ■■■

[Editors' note: Good, a London native, was a music producer, promoter, and manager who had done a number of rock 'n' roll-themed television programs in Britain. A pilot he shot led to the creation of Shindig, *which began in September of 1964 and lasted until January 1966. By that time, Good was no longer affiliated with the show.]*

■■ ■■■

Jack was always trying to get me to sing on the show or to be in a group he was forming called the Shindogs, which I was reluctant to do not only because of the research incident involving my Aries aunt but also because I considered that to be a most unfortunate and unlikely name for a group. Moreover, he wanted me to sing while walking slowly up a ramp so as to amplify my limp. Those cute, kinky English.

■■ ■■■

Editors' notes: Leon was born with cerebral palsy, which partially paralyzed the right side of his body, giving him his lifelong limp.

While Leon and other notable session players, including Glen Campbell and keyboardists Glen D. Hardin and Billy Preston worked in the Shindig house band, the Shindogs themselves are generally thought of as a quartet that included Leon's friend and fellow Tulsan Chuck Blackwell on drums along with James Burton on lead guitar, Joey Cooper on bass, and Delany Bramlett on guitar and vocals. Later, according to Blackwell, guitarist Don Preston joined up "and we went out and gigged," he told Wooley in the December 2003 interview. "We had a Top 10 [hit] up in Seattle. We used to go up there and play all the time."

In addition to appearing on the TV show and touring regionally, the Shindogs did some recording, scoring a minor hit with "Who do You Think You Are," produced by Leon for Viva Records, in 1967. There's more about Viva in the next chapter.

II III

A man named Bill Sargent was going to produce a rock show for TV and Jack Nitzsche was going to be the arranger and bandleader. I was looking forward to the project because it would have James Brown, Chuck Berry, the Rolling Stones, Marvin Gaye, and the Supremes, among others. Jack Good got wind of the project and made the announcement that anyone from the *Shindig* band who worked on Sargent's show would be fired. I stood up and said, "Thank you very much. I quit." I wasn't about to miss that show, and besides, I've never really been good with ultimatums.

II III

Editors' note: Leon refers here to The T.A.M.I. Show, *released by American International Pictures in 1964 as a theatrical feature rather than a television program. (T.A.M.I. is an acronym for either Teen Age Music International or Teenage Awards Music International—the movie has it both ways.) William H. "Bill" Sargent was the man behind a process called Electronovision, a process that used high-resolution two-inch video-tape that was transferred to film. Shot in Electronovision, The T.A.M.I. Show was assembled from concert footage taken at the Santa Monica Civic Auditorium on October 28 and 29, 1964.*

■■ ■■■

I had just bought a new Zeiss Ikon camera and spent the entire time documenting the event on 35mm film. Unfortunately, I was more avid photographer than archivist and many of the resulting prints were lost or stolen.

One of the things I did was follow James Brown and his spokesperson at a discreet distance so that I could hear the dialogue between them and the production team. James didn't say anything out loud the entire time; instead, he would whisper something to his lieutenant and the man would say, "Mr. Brown requires two follow spots at all times."

Further conversation revealed that Mr. Brown was not at all happy about going on before the Rolling Stones. "Mr. Brown always closes the show," said his man with a familiar authority.

At this time, James was not well-known by white audiences or white producers. I was concerned that the Stones would have their hands full after James came out and captivated the audience in just a few seconds with his normal agenda. I thought he would be impossible to follow—but the Stones played to nonstop cacophony.

When I watched them rehearse, I was surprised to see them sort of milling around the stage, except for a few points where it looked as though Mick and Keith were both running spontaneously toward the edge. When they played the show, the apparently spontaneous moves I'd seen in the rehearsal were repeated exactly in front of the audience, causing near-riot conditions. The finale included all the cast joining the Stones on the last number. Chaos ensued.

I didn't see the Stones again until years later, sometime after the Mad Dogs and Englishmen tour, when Mick asked me to arrange some horn parts for them for a session. I ran them down for him and he said, "That sounds like [the 1963 Bob & Earl hit] 'Harlem Shuffle.'"

I said, "I'm sorry. I thought that's what you did." What I meant by that was most of my experiences with the Stones up to that time had led me to believe they did their own versions of other people's licks.

They didn't use the parts, but they used [horn players] Bobby Keys and Jim Price for many years after that. I had introduced them at the session—which ended up costing me a thousand dollars. That was the amount the musician's union fined me because the Stones were not union members.

When the ABC-TV series *Shindig!* premiered on September 16, 1964, a Wednesday night, it was the first of its kind: a weekly, prime-time pop-music TV show whose performers didn't lip-sync their songs, as was the case on the same network's long-running daytime program *American Bandstand.* (An NBC clone of *Shindig!* called *Hullabaloo* came along four months later.) As suggested by the 1965 tie-in-magazine cover pictured here, *Shindig!* attracted many of the top rock and pop singers of the day.

Recommended by several music producers and his friend Jackie DeShannon, Russell was hired to assist in assembling the *Shindig!* house band—to be called the Shindogs—and to help in producing songs and backing the show's weekly guests. He put together what he considered to be the cream of the available L.A. musicians' crop: James Burton (lead guitar), Joey Cooper (rhythm guitar, vocals), Delany Bramlett (lead vocals, bass), and ex-bandmate Chuck Blackwell (drums), who had just returned from a record-smashing British tour with the Everly Brothers.

Shindig! lasted two seasons. Russell played in the band for most of the first season, occasionally playing a "spotlight" solo, before turning his piano chores over to Glen D. Hardin and leaving the show.

Courtesy of the Oklahoma Museum of Popular Culture/Steve Todoroff Collection.

Chapter Seven

CAN BE HARMFUL TO YOUR HEALTH

Snuff [Garrett] was head of A&R—21 years old; he was Liberty Records A&R Director. We had been there about a year, and he had already had hits with Bobby Vee, Johnny Burnette and Gene McDaniels. Snuff was hotter than a three dollar pistol. In 1962 Snuff had more hit records that he produced for Liberty than RCA had on their entire label.

—guitarist, performer, and music-industry figure Tommy Allsup, *in* The Flip of A Coin *by Guy Logsdon (Guy Logsdon Books, 2011)*

■■ ■■■

A **NOTHER CHARMER WHO** came into my life about this time [the mid-'60s] was a guy called Snuff Garrett. I spent some time wondering about a nickname derived from a tobacco product and decided it was a triumph of style over content, which was pretty much a road map for Snuff's agenda.

At the time we met, he was head of A&R for Liberty Records and in a lengthy slump as far as having any hits. He had uniquely unusual taste in music but was convinced that he represented the demographic for the majority of popular music. In all fairness, he had many hits to his credit, including practically all of the records done by Bobby Vee and Johnny Burnette and others. He had been one of the first young producers on the [late '50s-early '60s] Hollywood music scene and went through a run during which he seemed to be able to do no wrong.

I believe that I first worked with Snuff on an Everly Brothers session when he was having a little trouble. I can't really remember what the trouble was, but there was some arrangement or technical problem that was holding up the session. I had learned early in my Hollywood session work to keep my mouth shut and stay out of trouble, and this instance gave me a perfect opportunity to employ that philosophy.

I must have been amused as some aspect of the situation, though, because at one point, as I was observing it from the obscurity of my corner of the control room, Snuff looked in my direction and said, "Do you think you can do any better?"

I took the opportunity to fix the problem, whatever it was, and that incident became the basis of a relationship with Snuff that lasted a couple of years.

On the strength of that one Everly Brothers session, Snuff quit Liberty Records and formed Snuff Garrett Productions, with a logo that was a caricature of his face. At the time, Jerry Lewis, who was one of Snuff's Tinseltown favorites, had a logo in the same style. You can imagine Snuff's glee when Mr. Lewis's office called to talk to him about producing his son's band, newly formed and looking for direction.

Gary Lewis and the Playboys were a typical Bel-Air garage band, complete with endless blazers and equipment and the best production money could buy. It was not my cup of tea, but I was excited about the prospect of getting to make real records in a real studio for a real record company.

The first song Snuff found for the group was called "This Diamond Ring," written [with Bob Brass and Irwin Levine] by Al Kooper, who later went on to record with Blood, Sweat & Tears and other notable acts. The demo, sung by a soul singer in the R&B groove, was pretty good, and it was hard for me to make the transition in my mind from this great black vocalist to Gary Lewis. But I was striving to be a professional and I leaned into the work.

It was an exercise in dictation. I had to figure out parts that were simple enough to be played by the band and yet have some relationship to pop music. No mean feat, but after eight or ten hours of note-by-note dictation, the record was completed, for better or worse. I had installed my own lead vocal on the tape as a guide, and Gary would duplicate it, a couple of bars at a time.

A few weeks later, to my complete amazement, the record was soaring up the charts.

■■ ■■■

Editors' note: "This Diamond Ring," which made it to No. 1 (for two weeks) on the Billboard magazine pop singles chart, was the first of 15 hit records for Lewis and the Playboys, all coming between 1965 and 1969. (Lewis was drafted in the middle of this run, spending all of 1967 and most of 1968 in South Korea with the Army.) Leon arranged most of the hits and played on the records, along with other well-known West Coast session musicians who were members of the studio group later dubbed the Wrecking Crew. He also co-wrote the Top Five hits "Everybody Loves A Clown" and "She's Just My Style" and shared credit with Roger Tillison, another Tulsa expat, and Garrett on the 1966 Lewis hit "(You Don't Have to) Paint Me A Picture."

Leon also had something to do with the changing membership of the touring band, as former Tulsans Tom Tripplehorn (guitar), Carl Radle (bass), and Jim Keltner (drums), later replaced by another Tulsa drummer, Jim Karstein, took over for the original members.

Keltner, despite his Tulsa origins, didn't meet Leon until they were both in the Los Angeles area, where Keltner had moved with his family just as he was entering his teens. He was working in a music store and giving drum lessons when he met Gary Lewis, who eventually invited him to join the new band. Although jazz was Keltner's preferred musical idiom, he took the gig.

Here's Jim Keltner, talking about meeting Leon, in a July 6, 2012 interview with John Wooley:

Leon's hair was brown, and his beard was brown, and he was wearing a buckskin suit. I remember thinking, "Wow."

[Leon said] "Jimmy Lee, where yuh from?"

"I'm from Tulsa."

"Well, I'm from Tulsa, too."

He was quiet. Leon was real quiet, but very methodical, and I knew immediately he was a very serious music cat. Leon was actually the first real producer I ever worked for. Snuff Garrett, I guess you'd say, was the executive producer. Snuff was the big guy, and Leon was working for him as the record producer.

So we got in the studio, and the first thing we cut was that song "She's Just My Style" [the band's fourth hit, released in December 1965]. I didn't know what I was doing, but it was just instinctive. I'd already been playing some rock 'n' roll in these little bands I had, because we had to do some of that, so I could shuffle, you know. But my drums were tuned very tight. If you hear that song now, on the radio, my snare sounds very tight. I loosened it up later on. Carl Radle started teaching me about stuff: "Listen to this record, listen to that record."

Anyway, I played the little song, and Leon gave me a couple of pointers. He said, "On the fill here, on the front, can you do it backwards?" I said "sure" and played it backwards for him. He liked the fact that I could do that, and I remember he made a comment about it that made me feel good. And then he liked how I played the open hi-hat—I opened it for the intro. And based on those two things, he told me later on, "You could be a great rock drummer," or something like that.

And I remember thinking, "That's cool. If I only wanted to be a rock 'n' roll drummer."

But I remember feeling very complimented and very confident that I could do this. Within a week or so, I heard the record on the radio, driving around in my Corvette in Hollywood, and I was on top of the world.

■■ ■■■

I never really liked any of the Gary Lewis records and it was a painful period for me, but, again, I was trying to be a professional and not let any of my personal aesthetic considerations get in the way.

■■ ■■■

One day, Leon and I are sitting around and he says, "C'mon, Karstein. Let's run down to Wallichs Music City." It was at the corner of Sunset and Vine, an all-service music store. I liked to go there because they had a million 45's, and albums, and they sold sheet music and all kinds of *supplies. I think they even sold musical instruments. It was just a* wonderland, *you know.*

At this point in his life, I'm sure Leon had written out ten thousand chord charts. But chord charts are different than actually writing out a conductor's score, and actually scoring a whole session. So we run down there, and he goes over to the book section and buys a book by Henry Mancini on how to arrange [Sounds and Scores, *first published in 1962*]. *We go on back to the house, up to Skyhill, and he takes the book and stretches out on his bed and starts reading. About 20 minutes later I come in, and he closes it up and pitches it over in the corner; I think it's probably still there.*

Now, if he'd had to have scored 40 pieces with 12 strings and a choir for a Frank Sinatra session, he might've spent a little more time with it. But to arrange a Gary Lewis session—well, he didn't spend more than 20 minutes with that book.

—Jim Karstein, *from a November 22, 2017 interview with John Wooley*

Snuff was fond of saying, "If we could just keep you chained to a desk in the back room, we would make a fortune." Unfortunately, Snuff had a vague pronoun awareness, particularly as it related to "making a fortune."

One day, I told Snuff that I would like to do something as an artist. He suggested a string quartet, with piano and harpsichord, playing standards. He gave me a list of songs and I picked out the ones I knew and went to work on the arrangements, which took about two weeks. It was very stressful because I had never written for a string quartet before and didn't have a piano in my office.

When I was finished, I went to Western Studios and recorded the album in two days, using Johnny Vidor as quartet master. I had used him on many other projects and liked the sort of Gypsy quality he and his players seemed to come up with. They weren't what were considered the "first-line" players—that title being reserved for the string musicians who worked on film scores—but neither was I, so I felt right at home. Michel Rubini, who later became bandleader for Sonny & Cher, was my choice for piano. I played the harpsichord.

I was well-pleased with the album, as it was my first attempt at writing for a string quartet, so you can imagine my surprise when Snuff informed me that instead of using my name, as had been originally proposed, he was going to call the group the Midnight String Quartet. I was shocked and disappointed at this development, having visions of chains and desks and back rooms and vague pronoun awareness. The album stayed on the charts for 59 weeks and spawned a whole series of Midnight String Quartet discs—none of which I had anything to do with.

■■ ■■■

Editors' note: The album was 1966's Rhapsodies for Young Lovers, *released on Garrett's Viva label. It included arrangements of such soon-to-be-classic pop tunes as "Shadow of Your Smile," "Strangers in the Night," the Beatles' "Yesterday," and "Lara's Theme" from the 1965 movie* Dr. Zhivago.

A half-dozen records in the same style followed over the next couple of years, including a two-disc greatest-hits set. As Leon noted, he wasn't involved with any of them.

■■ ■■■

When I dissolved my association with Snuff Garrett, I was paid the equivalent of union scale for all the records I had made during the two years I was with him. I suppose it is possible to take the desire to cooperate too far. In this case, I think it cost me between seven and eight hundred thousand dollars.

As I look back at my life in Tinseltown, it is difficult to separate for the reader the interesting and amusing anecdotes from the sour grapes of destroyed expectations. Perhaps they are one and the same.

Russell (left) and producer Snuff Garrett (right), visit with Patti Lewis, wife of comedian Jerry Lewis, and her son Gary in this circa 1964 publicity photo. Through her company, Patti Lewis Enterprises, Mrs. Lewis was financing the sessions for her son's band, Gary Lewis and the Playboys, who had been signed to Liberty Records. The hit single "This Diamond Ring" came out of the first Lewis session, produced by Garrett and arranged by Russell.

Russell and Garrett later produced a session for Patti's husband featuring an orchestra and background vocalists, with a few lead vocals by Jerry himself. The group was dubbed the Jerry Lewis Singers and the album, *"Yesterday" and Other Folk Rock Hits*, came out in 1965 on the Dot Records label.

While Russell ended up having his issues with Garrett, the veteran producer recognized Russell's talent and, after leaving Liberty Records to form his own production company, asked Russell to join him.

"Leon was a musical genius, and his creativity was astounding," Garrett told Steve Todoroff in a 1983 interview. "During a break in one of the many Gary Lewis sessions we worked on, Leon went out and got a bass trumpet at a nearby pawn shop and came back in and added some incredible horn overdubs. It was one of the most amazing things I had ever seen."

Photo courtesy of Snuff Garrett. Used with permission.

Chapter Eight

ON THE ROAD TO XANADU

S OMEWHERE IN THE darkness of my past and quite contrary to the wishes of Nice Nancy Reagan [who created the "Just Say No" tagline for the Reagan administration's War on Drugs], I would "Just Say Yes." In fact, I practically never said "no."

In spite of all the questionable press received by Dr. Timothy Leary over the years, I would have to say that my first acid trip was the single most important event in my life. My vision and awareness were immediately expanded to 70mm Cinemascope and revelations were made to me that I previously hadn't even imagined. I think that is the main fear of the politicos and the liquor lobby: having to deal with the expanded awareness of a "turned-on" populace.

I have lost three good friends to drugs. Two are dead and the other is locked away for heinous crimes committed under the influence. Nevertheless, taking acid for the first time marked an important turning point in my life. Many charades of my own and others' manufacturing were stripped away at the speed of light, leaving a panic and fear that I am incapable of describing. I saw the face of a person I had considered among my closest friends, robbed of a veneer designed for the unaware, revealing a level of jealousy and hatred that makes me nervous to this day. In one 24-hour period I experienced indescribable ecstasies and pleasurable well-being, along with the most severe panic, fear, and insecurity of my life. I saw the auras that surround our species and, also, all the prejudiced opinions and hangups that I personally harbored, displayed in a neon fashion with a rapidity and unrelenting consistency that was certainly not for the faint of heart. It materially affected the course of my future life.

The first thing that happened after this experience was that I got on JJ Cale's motorcycle—the first time I had ever been on one—and immediately broke my hip trying to negotiate a very steep hill on the way to my house. Having visions of being run over by a car speeding through the blind intersection, I attempted to drag the cycle out of the way. Then I walked up the hill and leaned against a parked car, waiting for someone to come along and help me. After Jim Markham helped me up the stairs to my house, I went into shock and even the many quilts and an electric blanket barely overcame the intense feeling of coldness in my body. When I went to the hospital the next day, they discovered I had not only broken my hip, but also that it had reset itself during my walk up the hill.

━━ ━━━

We were living at Skyhill when acid came around. A lot of people we knew had taken it. We hadn't, but we kept talking about it, and he [Leon] wanted to do it. So we discussed it for maybe two weeks, and finally he decided to do it on a Saturday night, because he was off. That's when he was doing sessions, you know.

Amongst all the hype and everything about it, we'd heard that it was best to have someone there with you to guide you, that having an anchor would make the trip more of an experience. So, the big day came.

There wasn't a large crowd at Skyhill that night. In fact, I think it was him and me and [JJ] Cale, who was probably in the studio. So he took it, and it started taking effect, and he was enjoying it. There was never any bad trip involved. He was laughing and singing and doing the things you experience with acid. And he decided he wanted to ride Cale's motorcycle.

I kind of freaked out. I said, 'I'm not so sure that's a good idea." I mean, that was so unlike Leon. He'd never ridden a motorcycle in his life. But he finally convinced me he had to do it.

I said, "Well, I'm going to be right there with you."

Cale had a little 125cc motorcycle, and we got it fired up, and you might say it was an around-the-block experience. Skyhill was up in the hills in North Hollywood, sort of a neighborhood-ish situation, with the roads winding around, and there was hardly any traffic up there. So he went through that neighborhood on Cale's bike, and I walked along beside him and instructed the best I could, about the clutch and gears and all that. It wasn't like he was doing 50 miles an hour. He was kind of putt-putting along.

So he kind of went through the neighborhood and headed back up to 7709, to the house. Well, to the left it was very hilly, and there was one area up there where there was sort of a fall-off, down one side of the mountain. It wasn't like a canyon, *but it was steep. And he kind of stacked the bike up and fell off the side of that incline.*

I recall he thought he'd done something to his hip, and I think that was his polio hip. I went back and got Cale, because where Leon dumped the bike was just about, oh, a half-block from the house. Then I got Leon back home and that was kind of the end of it. He was dirtied up some, but I don't remember him going into any kind of shock. I'm not saying he didn't, *but I recall putting blankets on him, and I suppose he probably was in shock. I was just concerned that I was kind of responsible, even though I hadn't wanted him to get on that think in the first place.*

—singer-harmonica player Jimmy Markham, *from a January 2, 2018 interview with John Wooley*

■■ ■■■

At this time, I found myself wondering why I was associated with my then-current business partner. He was putting his name on every song I wrote, even though he didn't help write most of them. He reveled in psychologically debilitating would-be writers by listening to five or six seconds of their songs and saying, "No, that's not a hit." He offered his own arrogant, egocentric viewpoint as the standard of the music business. In general, he was a jerk and an all-around bore, to say nothing of the fact that he tried to keep me from attaining any success or even notice as a recording artist—even though I made most of the records for our company.

I was a lot less naïve after my experience with Dr. Leary's potion.

In further experimentation with elephant tranquilizer, commonly called angel dust or moon dust on the street, I had many mystical revelations and visions of a previous life. I was not quite sure I even believed in multiple lives and made a great effort to remember specific facts that I could check for accuracy at a later time. I saw myself as the king of the Persian Empire, complete with thousands of slaves and subjects. (I wonder why one never sees oneself as a car-wash worker in these types of visions?) The time frame was either 1100 years ago or 1100 years from some Persian starting point, such as the birth of Christ would be for Christianity. My name was Aram and my father's name was Abul.

I had many visions of different facets of my previous life, such as the time I had 3,000 subjects summarily executed because they had displeased me in some minor way. With later research, the only thing I was able to determine was that all the kings of Persia during that time had four letters in their names, which all began with the letter A.

Curiouser and curiouser.

One of the strongest visions I had during this period concerned a traveling beggar-musician, who came to my court and entertained for a while. I remember looking at him, watching him play and sing, and realizing that he lived in palaces with kings for his whole life but had no worries or concerns, such as the pressing business of state affairs that consumed most of my time. I saw myself in this life, a poor musician without any of the burdens I was then suffering as a head of state.

I also saw my own funeral. I was lying in a purple velvet room with ceilings that were so high as to be out of sight. Thousands of my subjects were passing by to pay their last respects.

I hesitate to admit these things and do so only because they actually happened to me.

I experienced a tremendous feeling of well-being from these visions, which lasted for several weeks. It was unlike anything else that was happening in my life.

During this period of time I also took 12 people to see Elvis at the Las Vegas Hilton.

Russell, hair-growing and mind-blowing, in a shot taken at his home on Skyhill Drive in July 1968. The era of his psychedelic recordings had begun about a year earlier and would continue into the '70s with such works as "Acid Annapolis" on the 1972 LP *Carney*.

Courtesy of Diane Sullivan. Courtesy of the Oklahoma Museum of Popular Culture/Steve Todoroff Collection.

Chapter Nine

THE ELVIS FACTOR

WHEN WE ENTERED the Las Vegas Hilton, a little tourist man looked forlornly at his wife and said, "Jesus," whereupon I raced over and said, "Yes! It's me! You've found me!"

Placing my hands on his head and shoulder, I entreated, loudly, "Heal him! Heal him!" Then, as he was melting into a heap of shock, I whispered, "Go in peace and tell no one you've seen me."

Because of that incident, I had a picture made at our table at the show, which I later printed up and titled "The First Supper."

I was wearing a white suit with white patent leather shoes, while my 12 companions were dressed in various hippie costumes. The sound that greeted us as we walked through the casino was that of a huge beast of a machine grinding to a halt—all the slot machines, roulette wheels, and other gaming activities came to a stop as we passed by.

I remember shouting, in the Pentecostal style, during the performance—"Touch the people, Elvis! Touch the people!"—my words inspired by the phenomenon of the many women going to the stage to receive a kiss or a scarf from the King. A lady at the table immediately behind ours kept saying to her son, "Avril, there's something going on here. There's something going on here." My enthusiasm wasn't in the least bit dampened by the bouncers, who kept coming over and asking, very politely, if I would hold it down a little. I couldn't help myself. I HAD COME TO SEE THE KING!

I spent the entire duration of that trip being completely in the world. Going up and talking to complete strangers, I would draw them out and discuss their problems, right in the middle of the casino.

I also attended Ike and Tina Turner's show, running up to the front of the stage and screaming answer notes to Tina as she sang. Somehow, I was able to hit any note I attempted so successfully that the bouncers and the audience thought it was part of the show. (Tina was looking a little rattled, though.) I have never done anything like that before or since, as that kind of behavior is completely outside my normal reality.

Another interesting thing about this trip was that I went up with about $350.00 in my pocket, picked up all the checks for 13 people during our three-day stay, and every time I was presented with a bill I handed the waiter or cashier all the money I had and then he or she went away and returned with change. I didn't gamble, and I didn't count the change I'd been brought until I got home. At that time, I discovered I had $650.00.

It smacks of loaves and fishes . . . curiouser and curiouser.

During another trip to Las Vegas, after meeting Elvis at the MGM Grand Hotel, I was a lot more forgiving of all the stupid things fans say when they approach their favorite stars in a state of nervous adoration. He called my name from the stage, said I was one of the best songwriters in the world, and sent word for me to come backstage for a meeting. After we were introduced by his piano player, Glen D. Hardin, I heard myself saying, "Elvis, how did you end up in all those horrible movies?"

You can imagine my horror. Yikes! Was that mild-mannered me saying that shit? I couldn't believe it.

He responded with much grace and without a moment's hesitation: "I don't know, man. The last thing I remember I was driving a truck."

I actually had wanted to know the answer to that question, on the level that I expected only greatness from one I perceived to be the greatest, but I was completely devastated that it had popped out of my unconsciousness without any help from me. I was unable to say anything else for the duration of the meeting. What fools these mortals be.

It is truly amazing the power that fame can bring. Mainly due to the efforts of [his Shelter Records partner] Denny Cordell, George, Ringo, Stevie Winwood, Bill Wyman and other famous people played on my first album [*Leon Russell*, 1970]. The first three or four days of recording with the stars went all right, mainly because I was able to get into the studio session-player mode I was very familiar with. I steamrolled my way through it without much thought beyond trying to keep it interesting for everyone and designing arrangements that would best spotlight the individual players. But after it was all over, I was in a state of complete disorientation and literally had to be led from the studio because I couldn't find my way out—even though I had been in and out of that very studio at least 20 times before. It took several hours to recover my senses.

The only other time I experienced this phenomenon was when Marjoe Gortner asked me to do a radio-preacher voiceover that would be heard over the radio during the trailer-house scene of the movie *When You Comin' Back, Red Ryder?* I wrote out a two-page narrative in the Pentecostal style, manufactured a cheap mike and amp setup, and read it like a hellfire preacher in the style of A.A. Allen. By the time I finished the second read-through, I was completely lost and totally disoriented. Roger Linn, my engineer at the time, had to show me out of my own studio. I didn't realize how high those preachers get, talking that way. It's a wonder I'm not right in there with Jim Bakker and Jimmy Swaggert.

∎∎ ∎∎∎

Editors' notes: When You Comin' Back, Red Ryder? *(1979) was produced by Gortner, a former child evangelist, who also took the lead role of a disturbed Viet Nam veteran whose car breaks down in a small town. Based on the Mark Medoff stage play of the same name, it co-starred Leon's fellow Oklahoman Candy Clark (born in Norman), known best for her work in 1973's* American Graffiti, *who was married to Gortner in 1978-79.*

Asa Alonso Allen (1911-1970) was a Pentecostal evangelist and faith healer who was one of the first preachers to establish a national television program. Biographical information indicates he was inspired to create his ministry after attending a 1949 tent revival held by Leon's fellow Tulsan, Oral Roberts.

The picture, taken at the Las Vegas Hilton, that Russell dubbed "The First Supper." The entourage waiting to see Elvis includes, from left, Joe Massot, Sandy Krasnow, Steve Bridges (Leon's cousin), Shady Adams, Mia Cordell, Emily Smith (in sunglasses), Russell, Kay Poorboy, Gram Parsons, Theodora Brinckman, Denny Cordell, and Clare Massot.

Photo courtesy of Barney Cordell. Used with permission.

Chapter Ten

ME AND JESUS

THINKING BACK TO the Jesus incident at the entrance of the Hilton reminds me of a couple of other times when this phenomenon occurred. One was in the very early morning at one of the first Willie Nelson Fourth of July Picnics. Although the show wasn't scheduled to start for seven hours, the crowd was already streaming through the many tall rock formations that surrounded the back of the natural amphitheater, which held the stage and space for an audience of about 60,000. I was sitting with Willie, watching this rather inspiring scene unfold, when he said, "I just figured it out. You're Jesus, and I'm John the Baptist."

I was a little shocked at the prospect, and I said, "No, no, not this time. *You* be Jesus this time."

I believe that his initial awe and esteem for me faded somewhat through the years, as he saw me, an idol he had placed on such a high divine pedestal, suffer from the many embarrassing foibles that plague almost everyone of our species.

There was another time that also included Willie, oddly enough. (Maybe he *is* John the Baptist.) [Percussionist] Ambrose Campbell and I were playing a concert with him in Detroit the night before Easter Sunday. I mentioned that the city was a hotbed of Church of God in Christ activity, and since there were probably Easter musicals going on all over town, we should try to find one to attend. The limousine was summoned and we made our way to the ghetto, searching for a COGIC Easter Pageant.

[Editors' note: The Church of God in Christ is a predominately African-American denomination formed in 1897, coming out of both the Holiness and Pentecostal traditions.]

■■ ■■■

It was about noon. The service was just ending at the first COGIC church we found, and I got out and walked over to a car where a man was sitting, his daughter of about four years in the back seat. Before the man even noticed my approach, the little girl looked out and shouted, "Jesus! Jesus!" and started trying to climb out of the back window into my arms.

Visibly upset by this turn of events, the young father tried, with some difficulty, to restrain his enthusiastic daughter from embarking on her crusade out the window. When I finally was able to ask him if he knew the location of any Easter musicals, he was not very helpful, and I went back to the limo to continue the search.

About a half-mile down the road we found a large COGIC church, with beautiful stained-glass windows and a parking lot filled with eight or nine hundred cars. As we entered, the eighty-voice choir was just finishing a rousing "Jubilee" and the offering was being prepared. When the sound level finally came down a little, I made my way up to the side of the pulpit and sat down by the organist on his bench, telling him about my quest for musicals.

"You're in luck today," he said. "The bishop of the whole Church of God in Christ is preaching at an auditorium downtown and there's supposed to be a 200-voice choir. I'm going to have to miss it because I have to play for choir practice this afternoon, but that is definitely the one to go to." He gave me directions, and off we went.

The service was supposed to start at one o'clock, and it was a pretty good distance to the auditorium, so we traveled quickly, hoping not to be late. As we arrived in the foyer, I took the opportunity to visit the lavatory and found two little boys in there, smoking cigarettes.

Looking at me, they said, "You the devil! You the devil!" and quickly doused their smokes, running out the door in mock alarm. When I rejoined Willie and Ambrose, I mentioned that it was quite an experience to be confused with both Jesus and the devil within fifteen minutes on an Easter Sunday.

We went inside and found the auditorium almost empty. I had forgotten that one o'clock on the COGIC agenda means somewhere between 2:30 and 3:00. We secured three seats exactly in the middle of the audience section as people slowly started arriving. After about 45 minutes, I noticed that the spectators had seated themselves in such a way as to leave a huge empty circle of seats surrounding us. There were people in front of us, to the sides of us, and in back of us, all in about equal numbers, but for a 25-seat radius in every direction, nothing but empty seats.

Noticing this, Ambrose said, "They are afraid of us, that's all. Don't worry."

It was only a few minutes later that an old couple left their seats in the first row and, Bibles in hand, marched up with much determination and authority and sat down right next to our unlikely trio. Ambrose, who was dressed in his own version of a bishop's costume, got up, turned to the two, and bowed deeply. Not one eye in the audience missed these proceedings, and within 15 minutes people from all over the section came to completely fill in what had been a circle of emptiness.

Just light one candle in the darkness.

Occasionally, when I'm on the road, I will construct "mojos" from material I pick up in the places I visit. On one occasion, I had made a rather spectacular necklace out of many crosses and a chain, material collected at the last 10 truck stops we'd been in. (Truck stops are magnificent places to find crosses of every description.) I was wearing it when I stopped for dinner at a particularly out-of-the-way rural diner in southern Georgia, taking a table inside with my first wife, Mary, and her two sisters, who were singing background for us at the time.

Seated next to our table were three ladies. After their order arrived, I noticed that one of the ladies was staring at me, constantly, her food going untouched. I thought perhaps she was having trouble with the idea of three black women sitting at a table with the likes of me, so I took the most fantastic cross off my necklace and handed it to her. She immediately burst into tears and was unable to eat any of her meal. Her sisters tried to console her for five minutes or so before deciding they would have to leave.

As she was on her way out, the lady gave me her personal Bible, with hand-written notations that looked like they covered 20 years, and said, "Your ministry will touch millions. Please take my Bible. It's all I have to give."

This, of course, brought peals of laughter from my wife and her sisters, but the lady didn't notice and neither did I, as I thanked her for the gift and told her to continue to love God.

Later, as we were leaving the small restaurant, I saw the same woman, sitting under a tree with her sisters, who were applying wet compresses to her head. Once we were inside our car, my wife laughingly proclaimed, "If she knew you as well as I do, she wouldn't be so impressed."

Whenever possible, my wife was fond of turning a beautiful and moving experience into a pile of shit.

I had often said I would marry a woman who was a better artist that I was but wouldn't beat me over the head with that fact. With this marriage, I was successful in doing only the former. The numerous knots and scars are still in evidence. I had visions of a family band that would travel the world, performing and writing music and not being separated by the many time and other demands that occur with people in show business. Instead, this marriage was a disaster of the first order that greatly damaged my self-esteem. The best laid plans of mice and men . . . .

(This is all beginning to sound too much like sour grapes, so back to the funny stuff.)

One afternoon I was flying to St. Louis with Emily Smith when I spotted, right in the first row of the first-class section, Dr. Billy James Hargis, a religious industrialist from Tulsa, who had fallen on hard times. His main evangelical efforts focused on a constant railing against the three most formidable weapons of Satan in our times: communism, rock 'n' roll, and homosexuality. However, only a few short months earlier, after he had performed a marriage ceremony for two students from his Christian school in Tulsa, something untoward had happened. Both of those students, on their wedding night, confessed to one another their sinful reality of having had sexual relations with Dr. Billy James.

The incident had been heavily reported in *Time*, a magazine in the style of the *National Enquirer*, only with better paper.

At this time I, by the sheerest coincidence, had found myself for the past week doing impressions of Ernest Angley, something I couldn't seem to shake. The opportunity to try them on Billy James Hargis was of the once-in-a-lifetime variety.

■■ ■■■

Editors' note: Billy James Hargis (1925-2004) was best known for his Christian Crusade *radio and television broadcasts from the early 1950s into the '70s, originating in Tulsa and espousing right-wing politics as well as fundamentalist Christianity over hundreds of stations. After founding American Christian College in 1971, he was forced to step down as president some three years later, following the alleged incident that Leon describes.*

Ernest Angley is another famous radio and television evangelist, broadcasting The Ernest Angley Hour *from his Ohio headquarters. He has also written a number of books. As of 2017, he was 93 years old and still preaching through his media empire.*

■■ ■■■

I got the opportunity I was looking for when Dr. Billy James approached our seats, about three rows behind his, and asked me, "Aren't you Leon Russell?"

"Why yes I am, Dr. Billy James, and what a perfectly wonderful pleasure it is to meet you, finally, in person," I replied, the voice of Ernest dripping ecclesiastically from my tongue.

"Leon, my son told me he saw you playing some *gos*-pel music somewhere," he announced, his perfect Pentecostal-evangelist brogue matching my own.

"Oh, yes, Dr. Billy James," I returned in my best Ernest. "You know I own the First Church of God at Third and Trenton." (Tulsa's First Church of God was currently in use as the Shelter Records recording studio.)

"You know, Dr. Billy James," I continued, "Satan is everywhere today, and he is out to do damage to the warriors of God at each and every opportunity. I want to tell you that you have a responsibility to keep a high profile in these trying times. God wants us to be strong in the face of any adversity that Satan might put in our path."

He said, "Well, Leon, in our bidness, people will try to hurt you if they can, and stop your good work. I've sold all my computers and my buildings and I've moved back to my little farm in Arkansas, where I have a little log chapel in the woods. I just go there and pray about my life and God gives me a blessing."

I had instantly progressed from a rock 'n' roll heathen to someone who, like Dr. Billy James, was in the "bidness."

"I have hired Jessup, out of Dallas, as a consultant for my new TV program," he continued, "and he told me that I need more 'jewry' and fewer interviews. He said they like 'jewry.'"

I was certain, somehow, that he was referring to the 14-carat-plated variety rather than to Zionists.

■■ ■■■

Editors' note: Here, Hargis is likely referring to the Reverend J. Charles Jessup, a popular preacher for decades (along with the aforementioned A.A. Allen) on radio station XERF, one of the flame-throwing broadcast outlets operating just across Mexico's border with Texas. According to Border Radio *by Gene Fowler and Bill Crawford (Texas Monthly Press, 1987), Jessup was arrested in 1964, charged with, and convicted by a U.S. judge of "fraudulent solicitation" of more than $10 million. They wrote:*

> *Jessup paid a few thousand dollars in fines, served a year in prison, and was on probation for five years, during which time he was forbidden to engage in self-promotion activities.*

With the indomitable spirt of a border blaster, however, Brother Jessup returned to the airwaves after his probation and preached the gospel regularly over XERF and other border stations to a small but faithful audience.

"Is this your lovely wife?" Dr. Billy James asked, gesturing toward Emily, who was sitting beside me and trying hard to maintain a somber countenance. She was achieving this with some difficulty, having wet her pants as she tried to keep from laughing during my "high profile" and "trying times" speech.

"Oh, no, Dr. Billy James," I told him. "This is my secretary, Emily."

He nodded, but apparently, my announcement fell on deaf ears, as he continued to refer to Emily as my "lovely wife" throughout the rest of the conversation.

"Leon," he said, "I want you and your lovely wife, Emily, to have this little New Testament I was taking home to my wife, and I want to write a scripture down here in the front for you to read when you get time."

We were, as I mentioned, heading away from Tulsa to St. Louis at the time, so his statement about its being a gift for his wife wasn't altogether convincing. Plus, the special New Testament was embossed with the words "Dr. Billy James Hargis Ministries, Tulsa, Oklahoma," just like the ones he offered on his television show.

The scripture passage he wrote down was from Romans, and Emily and I labored over it for quite some time, trying to find a connection to any part of the conversation we'd had with Dr. Billy James.

When we disembarked at the St. Louis airport we howled at such great lengths and with such volume and enthusiasm that we piqued the interest of a passing security guard, who suggested we take our mirth into the cocktail lounge.

About a month later, we received a personal letter from Dr. Billy James, telling us what a pleasure and inspiration it was to meet me and my "lovely wife, Emily," and inviting us to his farm and little chapel in the woods for a three- or four-day stay whenever it was convenient for us.

We were never able to accept that invitation, but that meeting on the plane to St. Louis remains one of the high points of my life.

An outtake from the photo shoot for the picture sleeve of the 1974 Shelter Records single, "If I Were A Carpenter," with Russell posing as Jesus Christ. Through his years of recording and performing, religion and spirituality were important to Russell, whether in the self-described "artificially induced religious experience" quality of his early shows or in songs he wrote and/or recorded, including "Roll Away the Stone," "Jesus Will Take Me Home," and the unreleased "Lilies of the Field." *A Mighty Flood*, released in 2006 by his Leon Russell Records label, was a whole album of gospel songs.

Russell was a fan of *The Urantia Book*, a famous spiritual and philosophical work aimed at uniting religion, science, and philosophy. He claimed that the numerous references to "paradise" within that text inspired him to start his Paradise Records label in the mid-'70s.

Toward the end of Russell's career, his references to religion and the Almighty seemed to increase. An example of this was the addition of "His Eye Is on the Sparrow" to his live shows.

Photo by Dan Mayo. Used with permission.

Chapter Eleven

GIMME SHELTER

IN 1969, I WAS CONTACTED by an employee of A&M records who told me that Denny Cordell was coming to the U.S. from England to record Joe Cocker, and that, after hearing my piano on the Delaney and Bonnie album [*The Original Delaney & Bonnie & Friends,* released earlier in the year], he was interested in having me play on the project. It was an exciting prospect for me, as I very much liked "With A Little Help from My Friends," the title track of Joe's first album, which Denny had produced.

Joe's Grease Band, with Chris Stainton on keyboards, was scheduled to record with him, so I wasn't quite sure why they needed me. Still, I was excited at the invitation.

██ ███

"Little Help from My Friends" sort of took off in America . . . as a single, and we had the opportunity to go over to America because Joe's booking agency handled Steve Winwood and several other groups. . . .

It was a nine o'clock flight and we had to be at Heathrow airport at 7:30 in the morning. Everybody thought we'd better stay together at the same house. We were extremely jacked-up, as you can imagine. It was every English rock 'n' roller's dream to go to America . . . . So we meet at [Grease Band drummer] Bruce Rowland's house, because he's closest to the airport. We all arrive there in the evening, and Joe comes in and he's bought a record.

We used to buy our records at a record store called Musicland. A guy named Reg Dwight was the counterboy. Joe had gone down there to see what was on and Reg had given him this record and said, "Take this one. You gotta check this one out. You won't believe it!" Of course, as everybody knows, Reg Dwight went on and became a piano player-vocalist by the name of Elton John.

This will give you some idea how far that connection between Elton and Leon goes back. Elton sold Joe the record where we [first] heard Leon.

[Joe] comes back to the flat and puts this record [The Original Delaney & Bonnie & Friends] *on and it totally, I mean completely, blew us away. The sound of the piano—we listened to it all night long. We never did go to sleep. We were afraid we'd miss the plane, so we stayed up all night, listening to that record.*

We met Denny Cordell at the airport in London the next morning, and the first thing we said was, "Denny, we've got to meet this incredible piano player, Leon Russell." When we arrived in New York and Denny had made sure we were all set, he took off to Los Angeles to find Leon Russell, because we wanted to know who he was and we wanted to work with him.

—Former Joe Cocker road manager Peter Nicholls, *from a July 20, 1987 interview with Steve Todoroff and Brian Thompson*

II III

When I first dropped by Sunset Sound [in Los Angeles], where the Cocker sessions were to take place, I found much sitting around going on, the studio liberally sprinkled with ganja and prime hash in huge blocks, sporting the seal of the government of Morocco. (Those Arabs really know how to have a good time, don't they?) After I had been there for about two hours, the situation maintaining absolute continuity, I started to get a little nervous. I was from the Hollywood school of union record-making, where you were expected to cut three songs in the allotted three-hour session, no matter what. All I could see what the $200 per hour studio tab, plus the $1,500, or more, three-hour bill for the musicians.

I kept leaving, and coming back, and somehow, records were made. (Denny later told me he had gotten into the habit of making records this way when he was back in England, where studio time cost the equivalent of a couple of hundred dollars a day and the session musicians cost about $50 for a 10-hour period.)

We eventually moved to A&M Studios, where we cut "Delta Lady" and another song I had written called, "Hello, Little Friend." I was used to recording in my own home studio, designed by my friend Bones Howe, the engineer on many of the records I had made while I was in partnership with Snuff Garrett. The idea of my having a home studio was inspired by the brilliant TV comedian Ernie Kovacs, who had a studio in his own house, and also by Les Paul, the inventor of multi-track recording.

I told Denny I would have to take the tape to my house before I could really tell what was going on, so, after the A&M sessions, we headed out to Skyhill Drive, near Universal City, where my home and studio were located. It was late when we arrived, but everyone was anxious to hear the completed record, so we went to work.

I was used to dealing with tape under a microscope, overdubbing and inserting parts and generally repairing anything that might have been a mistake, or something ill-conceived in the recording. At first, the process was difficult on this particular project, because Denny and Joe kept up a constant commentary about how this or that didn't sound quite right, or this part seemed wrong. I explained I was dealing with component parts of the sound, and that it was premature to judge at this point. Asking them to please let me finish the whole process, I told them the time would come when their commentary would be timely and, if they didn't like something, I could fix it then.

After the work was done, everyone seemed to be happy and Cordell later told me he had never seen any plastic surgery more successfully accomplished.

■■ ■■■

[Editor's note: In addition to playing on the Joe Cocker! *LP, Leon is credited as an arranger and co-producer.]*

■■ ■■■

The next day we met at A&M and discussed starting Shelter Records. I told Denny my ideas about label identification, in the style of the early Atlantic Records, where you knew that if you bought anything with that label on it you would get good music. I also mentioned that I thought it would be a good idea to hire a person who would be a living advertisement for the record company, having in mind someone like a Colonel Sanders. At the time, I guess I didn't realize who the obvious candidate was for that position.

Denny Cordell was the first business-oriented person I ran into in Hollywood who actually dug my chili. I had spent time making overtures to Herb Alpert, Bobby Darin, and others I'd worked with, trying to get them to recognize my potential as a solo artist, but for some reason they all seemed to be on a different wavelength. Cordell, who was a fan of mine, reckoned they were just not rock 'n' rollers. (Who would have thought?)

He had a singular style all his own. When he found out I had an Asylum Choir record in the can at Mercury, he borrowed the necessary money and bought the master with cash. I will never forget the nervous expression on the Mercury man's face as Cordell laid out 200 one-hundred-dollar bills on the desk, picked up the tape, and left the office.

■■ ■■■

[Editors' note: Made up of Leon and guitarist Marc Benno, the Asylum Choir debuted with 1968's Look Inside the Asylum Choir, *released by Mercury subsidiary Smash Records. The second and final disc from the duo is the one Leon refers to here. It was released by Shelter as* Asylum Choir II *in 1971.]*

■■ ■■■

Denny's ability to communicate his past achievements was a delight and a wonder to behold. Many times I saw and heard him relate sales figures to a potential investor or distributor without missing a beat, recalling the chart positions for perhaps 20 singles and ten albums with all the attendant accounting that is of interest to people of that type. Once, he fell on the floor in mock exhaustion outside the door of a particularly powerful music-company head.

Part of my first album was recorded in England. Denny arranged for many English stars to appear on the record, which was, as far as my knowledge of the music business goes, the first time that had happened [with an American act]. He secured the services of Glyn Johns, who had been an engineer on many of the early Beatles records. It was exciting indeed.

Ringo and George were both on the first sessions, and it was incredible how Ringo could immediately play back the drum parts I sang to him. (You'd think he'd been working with Paul McCartney.) At one point, John and Yoko came in and watched the proceedings for several hours, sitting on the floor of the studio. George was a pleasure, constantly lending support and enjoying the whole event so much.

The next day it was Bill Wyman and Charlie Watts who, along with Steve Winwood, played on "Roll Away the Stone." I was interested in making a Rolling Stones-type record of that song, and those were just the guys to do it. On one I called "Prince of Peace," Glyn contacted Eric Clapton to play slide acoustic guitar. I was higher than the proverbial kite at the prospect of playing with these great artists I had admired so much from a distance.

After about five days, we returned to Wally Heider Studios in the States to finish and dub down. I had been completely enthralled by the whole process, and I will be forever grateful to Denny for launching my career as a solo artist.

Russell and the man who "dug his chili"—Denny Cordell—at Cordell's home in Sherman Oaks, California, 1970. After their first meeting, the man from England and the man from Tulsa established such a great connection that they made plans to form their own record label (Shelter Records) and publishing company (Cordell-Russell Music), and to record Russell as a solo act.

In Russell, Cordell found the perfect artist: a seasoned musician, singer, songwriter, arranger, and producer. In Cordell, Russell had someone who not only believed in his abilities, but also had years of experience in the business side of the music industry. Their partnership would last for some seven years.

Photo by Linda Wolf. Used with permission.

Chapter Twelve

MAD DOGS AND ENGLISHMEN

IMMEDIATELY AFTER THE Elvis trip to the Vegas Hilton, Denny Cordell arrived at my house on Skyhill Drive, with a very dismal Joe Cocker in tow. Joe had been booked for a 45-day tour by the Premier Talent Agency in New York, but he had fired his band back in England the day before he and Denny had left for L.A. Now, with only six days before the tour was scheduled to start, the musicians' union had let Joe know that if he didn't play those shows, he would never work in the United States again.

He wanted to know if I could help him put a band together.

After thinking about it for a minute or two, I realized it wouldn't be that difficult to do. Most of the musicians I'd played with in one configuration or another were available and would be happy to go on the road. So I said yes.

The first person I called was Chuck Blackwell, whom I had played with for years in Tulsa. Then Carl Radle. I had rescued Carl from an uncertain fate at Seismograph of Tulsa by getting him on the Gary Lewis band (an even more uncertain fate). After that I phoned my friend Don Preston, the first white guy I'd ever known who could play like B.B. King.

Those calls took all of 15 minutes, after which time I reported to Joe that the principal rhythm section was in place and that I had some other ideas about the tour, if he was interested. Starting to get a little color back, he asked me to continue. I said I thought it would be a good idea to hire news photographers as cameramen, get a large cast of choir singers and extra musicians to be in the show, and create a documentary-style movie of the entire event. I told him that because of the enlarged production cost the tour wouldn't make much by itself, but it would finance the movie, which had a chance of making a lot of money. I wanted a private airplane for the concert and movie crew, who would film everything that happened both on and off the stage, giving an insight into the hippie culture that was flourishing in America at the time. I thought it was important that all the cast and crew eat at least one meal together each day, to have an opportunity to discuss the latest events and, in general, to weld the consciousness of all concerned into one common awareness.

It was the first time in my life that I had laid out an idea with all the components documented by a secretary, who sat quietly taking notes in the corner. Everything was agreed to by Denny and Joe and we were on our way into musical history.

The next day, I had my crew—which consisted of all the people I'd taken to see Elvis in Vegas—go out and buy several 30-gallon galvanized trash barrels, and we began to make potato salad and baked beans in quantities that could've fed the cast and crew of *Cleopatra*. *[Editors' note: Here, Leon refers to the 1963 epic movie starring Elizabeth Taylor, notorious for its huge budget and cost overruns.]* At that time, the sound stage at A&M Records wasn't being used for much, and we converged there the next day at three o'clock, trash barrels full of food, to start rehearsals. I don't remember specifically what happened, but I looked around on the third day and there were 25 people in the band and chorus and about 300 looking on, including Herb Alpert [musician and A&M co-founder], who asked if I could put a rhythm section together for him. He told me he thought I was the kind of guy who just sat in rooms and wrote things down on paper.

■■ ■■■

[Joe Cocker's manager, Dee Anthony] said, "You've got to tour."
Joe said, "No. We're not. Besides, we don't have a band anyway."
He said, "You're going to tour, or the musicians' union will throw you out of the country and revoke your visas."

That's all he had to say, because we'd only just moved to this country. So we went to Leon and said, "What are we going to do?"

So Leon says, "That's no problem. I've got a lot of friends, and we'll put together a band for you."

And Joe says, "Okay. Let's give it a try."

We went down to A&M Studios and we had five people the first night: Carl Radle, [drummer] Jim Gordon, Chris Stainton, Leon, and Joe. I put some equipment together for them and they played. The next night, a couple more folks came down. By the end of the week there were about 15 people blowing away on stage.

So all of a sudden, it started to develop. We got the horn players, Bobby Keys and others, and it all started to build up until we had a nucleus of about 15 people, and the band just sounded incredible! You would not have believed it. I mean, a week or so before, no band at all, and then . . . .

—Peter Nicholls, *from the 1987 interview with Todoroff and Thompson*

■■ ■■■

Most of the people who ended up in the cast were hired out of the audiences that came to the rehearsals. Bobby Jones, who was a bass player and singer [and a former member of rock 'n' roll pioneer Gene Vincent's Blue Caps] with a good rock 'n' roll look, was hired to sing in the chorus. So was Claudia Lennear, an ex-Ikette, complete with beautiful dancer's legs and a Tina Turner wig. Jim Gordon and Rita Coolidge came to watch the rehearsals and asked to be on the show. Since most of the songs on my first album had been written about them, I felt I couldn't refuse. Besides, Rita was a beautiful singer and Jim was the most proficient studio drummer I had ever worked with at the time.

Jim Keltner, who had been introduced to me by Gary Lewis, came in and wanted to be on the show. I couldn't refuse him; he is a unique and truly unusual player. [Drummer] Sandy Konikoff, from Buffalo, New York, had his own particular contribution to make. Bobby Keys and Jim Price called and begged to be in the horn section, but I was reluctant to use them because they were, I thought, playing at the time with Delaney & Bonnie. They assured me that they had just quit and it wouldn't interfere with anything if they went on the tour. [Vocalist] Donna Washburn, another of my old friends, was also added to the choir, along with the Moore brothers, Matthew and Daniel, and a pretty girl with a cute spotted dog, whose names both escape me.

I was going to play guitar, so I asked Chris Stainton, from Joe's ill-fated Grease Band, to play organ. I'm not quite sure why he, of all the Greasers, came to America with Joe, but he was a welcome addition to the group.

Time was short, and I tried to think of songs we could play that we all knew in order to pull this thing off in the small amount of time we had. The audience was going to expect Joe's hits, but we needed other songs to fill out a two-and-a-half hour program. When I would think of one, I would ask Joe if he thought it was a good idea—and not get much response. We would rehearse it a bit and I would ask if the arrangement sounded right to him. Whereupon, he would always say, "I guess it never sounds right to me."

I was used to working with clients who had strong opinions about everything, so it was a new experience not to have that kind of feedback. Finally, I decided I would just do whatever I wanted, and if he didn't like it he could tell me. Later, when I saw the movie and heard him make the remark about how he would stick his head in a toilet if someone told him to do it with enough conviction, I thought the line was probably a coded accusation that I had made him do something he didn't want to do. The truth was, it was very difficult to get him to offer an opinion about *anything*.

Near the end of the rehearsals, the production staff started to arrive in the form of Peter Nicholls, who had worked as Joe's production manager, and [tour manager] Sherman "Smitty" Jones, a very colorful procurer of female entertainment, who was forever organizing meals, ordering wine, reciting Shakespeare, and recounting stories of his adventures with Frank Sinatra. I later traded him my fake Patek Phillipe watch for his Swank model, which he accepted with much enthusiasm. It also made me happy. As part of the bargain, he threw in one of his girls for an evening.

The *Mad Dogs and Englishmen* tour was a complete and absolute success, covered by *Time* and *Life* magazines and documented, more or less, in a movie. I wanted to edit the film myself, but Denny Cordell convinced me that I should go out on the road and support my own solo album, which had just come out as the first release on our Shelter Records label. Also, he kept telling me that I was going to be accused of "career profiteering," and I would be well-served to limit my association with the final cut.

I didn't know what he was talking about. We had over 200 hours of raw footage that had to be assembled into an hour-and-a-half feature. To this day, I believe that if A&M hadn't so shamelessly pursued a PG rating for the movie it would've been the definitive document for a whole generation and a huge success as a movie. This was not to be.

After the tour, Joe returned to about the same situation he'd been in before, in that he had no band. He sort of spent his time getting drunk at Cordell's house in Encino for the next six months.

II III

Joe used to look at me—you can see it in the movie, in fact, if you watch it from this point of view. . . . There's a scene in the movie where he and I . . . are talking to each other about fantasy, right, of how we got started, how we learned our moves. When I look at it, I can see him looking at me like, "What are we doing here with these guys?"

We never meant it to be that way at all. . . . We wanted a band, but when you get into something like that, you can't stop it. I mean, you just go with it. But if your name was on the marquee, what are you going to do now? What do you do next? I mean, it wasn't The Leon Russell Show, it was Joe Cocker and Mad Dogs and Englishmen.

So he's sitting there at the end of the tour going, "Now what am I going to do? Now I'm really in trouble." He just had no direction. And everybody's buzzing around and everybody's telling him this and telling him that . . . . It was really distressing because he obviously didn't know what to do.

—Peter Nicholls, *from the 1987 interview with Todoroff and Thompson*

II III

I finally got the picture on "career profiteering" when *Rolling Stone*, the magazine, started reporting—in what I'm sure was a completely objective series of articles—that I had a "Svengali" hold on Cocker and had caused him to be now unable to perform. Also, according to the reports, I had created the Mad Dogs and Englishmen tour according to my own devious agenda and was standing on Joe's neck to further my own career.

I wasn't bothered by those stories very much because, at that time, I considered Joe to be a true friend. So I knew at any moment he was going to come to my rescue and put the nasty rumors to rest. Unfortunately, he handed the situation in the same style he'd handled the rehearsals. He said nothing.

When Joe continued not working, people started showing up from Joe's [booking] agency with tape recorders, asking me why the tour didn't make any money, why there were $18,000 tabs for wine and booze for the tour dinners, why Joe wasn't performing any more, and was I ashamed of the way I had ruined his career?

I explained that I didn't drink wine or anything else on the tour; that the alcohol was ordered by Smitty when he set up the meals. And as for ruining Joe's career—I still felt that he would come forward and tell how I had helped him in a tough time.

To this day, he has not done that. Too many toilets and too little conviction.

As the saying goes, if I had it to do all over again, I'd do it all over you. If I had had any idea of the abuse I would receive from the press about *Mad Dogs and Englishmen*, I'm afraid I would have taken a different road. One must never rule out the attraction of industrial plumbing and pipefitting.

Russell and Joe Cocker onstage during the *Mad Dogs and Englishmen* tour, circa 1970. Threatened by the musicians' union with disbarment from the U.S. if he didn't go through with a planned tour, and without a band, Cocker was desperate when he and manager Cordell visited Leon at Skyhill Drive. The group Russell put together for Cocker, as well as the *Mad Dogs* tour, elevated Russell's standing in the rock world while allowing him to play out the fantasies of performing he'd had since his early youth.

Photo by Linda Wolf. Used with permission.

Chapter Thirteen

GEORGE HARRISON

SOME TIME AFTER the English sessions for my first album, I visited George Harrison's estate in Henley-on-Thames, which was also the site of the world-famous boat races. The house had been constructed by a barrister, starting in about 1875 and continuing for a period of 26 years. The structure is a complete send-up of the Catholic Church, done in the classical style of the period, with all the statuary and relief carvings done as a heavy, if subtle, satire of the Church. There were beautiful stone carvings of monks high on the outside of the building, one for each section of the house; one I remember in particular is the Monk of the Kitchens, a singularly nasty-looking figure, holding a baby by one leg. The baby's head is in its large, grotesque mouth.

The rest of the statuary was equally colorful. As the story goes, any architectural tradesman who came to Henley needing work was invited to participate in the massive construction project—an elegant soup kitchen of sorts.

Upon the death of its owner and builder, the estate was given to the Catholic Church for use as a convent. After 50 years, George bought it from Church officials. The only changes the good sisters had made had been to put plaster of Paris over the genitalia of all the elegantly carved statues and sell most of the elaborate chandeliers and wooden carvings from inside. In spite of that, it is still the most remarkable house I have ever seen. The Biltmore Mansion in Asheville, North Carolina, pales by comparison.

:: :::

[Editors' note: Biltmore House, touted in advertising as "America's largest home," was constructed by tycoon George Washington Vanderbilt II during the Gilded Age of the late 1800s.]

:: :::

After we "just said yes" to a Jamaican-sized portion of the Holy Moroccan ganja, George treated us to a tour of the quasi-dungeons that ran for about a mile underneath the house. They started out with many cells constructed of steel, jail-type bars, complete with torture equipment and chains with metal cuffs, all satires of the types really used in the dungeons of the period. From there, the tunnels deepened until they held four or five feet of water. Originally, they had supported small boats in a sort of tunnel-of-love motif. Wearing galoshes, we waded through the water and mud to a point where the tunnels opened onto a pristine lake. George walked out across it, on top of the water, in the style of Peter Sellers' character in the movie *Being There*. Given the state I was in, I was convinced I was with a true extraterrestrial. As it turned out, the lake was made of concrete and the water was only one-and-a- half inches deep.

The landscaping of the property was remarkable. George had five gardeners at that time, all working constantly to maintain and improve the plantings. It was possible to stand in a certain section of the property and feel that you were in Colorado, then move 30 feet or so and get the impression you were in a rural deer park in Japan, complete with rock garden and tea house. The estate is prominently featured in one of George's videos and on an album cover. *[Editors' note: Here, Leon is possibly referring to the cover of 1970's* All Things Must Pass, *Harrison's first solo LP after the breakup of the Beatles.]*

Later, [in the summer of 1971], George called me to his house in [L.A.'s] Benedict Canyon and said he was considering doing a benefit for the refugees of Bangladesh as a favor to his close friend and teacher, Ravi Shankar. *[Editors' note: At the time, the Bangladesh War of Independence was raging throughout the country, with millions of civilians caught between the warring forces.]* By then, the Beatles had been off the road for several years, and George was a little apprehensive about appearing in public again. I told him I felt that his fans were still out there, dying for a glimpse of him and a chance to hear his voice. I had no doubt that the audience response would be incredible, especially after he told me that Eric Clapton was set for the event and Ringo had also committed. He was trying to get Bob Dylan to appear, and he wanted me to put the band together. That night, he wrote the ballad "Bangladesh." A few weeks later, we were on our way to Madison Square Garden.

The rehearsals only lasted about two-and-a-half days, with Bob Dylan arriving at the last minute of the second day. He watched the rehearsals for a good while, appearing to be uncertain about whether to play solo or with the large band. After much coaxing from George, he finally got on the stage and sang a song or two by himself. Then, he asked George and me to join him. George, of course, played electric guitar, and I played bass, something I had just done on Bob Dylan's "Hurricane" record. We tried a song or two, and then I suggested that Ringo join us on tambourine.

That would be his band for the performance.

We rehearsed a few songs, figuring out the arrangements, but when we all came out for the actual show, he played the song we'd rehearsed in 4/4 time as a waltz. The rest of us sort of stood there for a moment, until we figured out what was happening, and then we joined in.

I have never seen such a complete metamorphosis take place in any other human being. When Bob Dylan was offstage, he looked like an ordinary guy. But as soon as he reached the back of the stage, he changed drastically. I can't put into words what happened that day, but when he took the stage his presence became all-powerful.

We did two shows, one in the afternoon and one in the evening, and he was noticeably more relaxed in-between than he had been before the first concert. In fact, as he was sitting there holding his guitar, I took the opportunity to request all my favorite Dylan songs. He played about 20 of them in a row for me before saying he had to go get ready for the second show. I had just gotten quite a show myself.

Before the evening concert started, he called me over and asked if I thought the second audience would be like the first.

"In what way?" I asked.

"In any way," he replied.

"Well," I said, "there will be 20,000 people again, and they will all know who you are and know all of your songs. I guess from that standpoint they will be pretty much the same."

He seemed pleased with my opinion as we headed out to do the second show. Because Bob Dylan had been a powerful influence on me and materially changed my mind about many aspects of music and poetry, it was a great pleasure to appear with him on that stage. Playing with him and the others was a singular high point in my life.

After the concerts were over, I commented to George that it was unfortunate we had to now spend all the money we'd raised for Bangladesh. Estimating that the revenues generated from the live performance and the subsequent records and movie would generate $20 million, I suggested we should form a foundation that included the performers and others, perhaps headed by [famed architect and visionary] Buckminster Fuller. If we only spent the interest that the money generated, not the principal, and did one or two concerts a year, we could produce a fund in the billions within a few years, providing interest income for many different charitable needs.

George contacted our mutual friend Al Aronowitz [the music journalist best known for introducing Dylan to the Beatles], who was a writer for the New York *Post* at the time, and sent him to Washington D.C. for a meeting with Bucky to see if he had any ideas on the subject. Al returned with the news that Mr. Fuller had said he could build, for one million dollars, temporary housing out of rolled newspapers that would provide shelter for 250,000 refugees. Concerned about whether this could actually happen, George didn't pursue the idea further. Instead, the money for Bangladesh was distributed through UNICEF, and that was that.

Throughout his life, Buckminster Fuller was plagued with a lack of confidence from his potential supporters, something that has defeated other great visionaries throughout the ages.

George Harrison practices for the *Concert for Bangladesh* event. Instrumental in lining up the musicians and singers for the benefit concert, Russell always considered playing on stage with major influences like Harrison and Bob Dylan a high point of his career.

Harrison and Russell first got together in the fall of 1969 when Denny Cordell, then Russell's partner in Shelter Records, took Russell to London to record at Olympic Studios. Apple Records' Chris O'Dell, who had taken a fancy to Russell, was assembling musicians for an album by Jackie Lomax and let Harrison and Ringo Starr know that Russell would love to have them play on the Olympic session. Both ex-Beatles agreed, and on Russell's first solo disc, 1970's *Leon Russell*, they became part of an international all-star aggregation.

Photo by Don Nix. Courtesy of the Oklahoma Museum of Popular Culture/Steve Todoroff Collection.

Chapter Fourteen

MY LIFE WITH AMBROSE

Editors' note: Born Oladipupo Adekoya Campbell in 1919, Nigeria native Ambrose Campbell ended up in Britain soon after the beginning of World War II. He was instrumental in forming several bands there, including the West African Rhythm Brothers, who have been cited as England's first-ever all-black musical group. In 1972, he came across the Atlantic with Denny Cordell, who introduced him to Leon.

Ambrose returned to Britain in 2004 to be with family, dying there two years later at the age of 86.

■■ ■■■

AMBROSE CAMPBELL WAS introduced to me by my partner in Shelter Records, Denny Cordell, in response to a comment I had made about how I'd like to meet an African drummer. He is that and much more. Since our meeting in 1972, he has been with me constantly, playing in all my different performing configurations. He first played with the Shelter People and then with the GAP Band tour, which came after the release of the first Hank Wilson album [1973's *Hank Wilson's Back*, featuring Leon as his country-music alter-ego.] He was also with me when I toured with my wife Mary and later, with the New Grass Revival.

Ambrose comes from a well-known family in Lagos, Nigeria. The city has a prominent park named Campbell Square which was named after his grandfather, who was what might be called a witch doctor by "civilized" society. The grandfather, wanting Ambrose's father to have every advantage and opportunity, sent him to school in England, where the man lived for many years. He returned to Nigeria as a Christian minister, telling his dismayed father that his "heathen" religion no longer applied and was not worship of "the one true God." This was very disappointing to the old man, as he'd had hopes of passing his extensive knowledge of mystic religious rituals and healing to his off-spring. It was not to be. The work of the English teachers of religion had erected a barrier that neither father nor son would breach. As a result, Ambrose received all of the teachings that his grandfather had planned to hand down to his father.

Ambrose told me of an incident in which his father requested that he, Ambrose, be a liaison between him and Ambrose's grandfather. "Ambrose," he said, "my father is making me look a fool. Here I am, a bishop in the church, and my own father holds onto superstitions and heathen beliefs that make me a laughingstock. The people don't trust me and won't come to my church. You must ask him to come to my service."

Carrying out his parent's wishes, Ambrose went to his grandfather with the request. The old man was not interested in participating in "the charades of the white man" that had been responsible for his own son taking the wrong road, but, as a favor to young Ambrose, he agreed to attend.

All was going well until near the end of the service, when the old man started singing the traditional songs of the Yoruba religion. That, along with a few incantations, filled the sanctuary with a stampede of frightened parishioners.

After it was all over, Ambrose's father asked the old man, "Why do you insist on embarrassing me in front of my congregation? I am not a bishop. I am the laughingstock of the village."

The grandfather smiled and drew a line in the dirt in front of the village church. Pointing to it, he said, "Take your white man's Bible and come across this line."

Visibly irritated by his father's antics, the bishop reluctantly took up his Bible and approached the line. But the closer he got to it, the more he slowed, until it seemed he was walking in molasses. Before he could cross, he came to a complete stop. He turned around and tried again—with the same result.

"Ambrose," said the bishop, sounding confused. "You come try this."

Ambrose told me that as he approached the line, Bible in hand, it was as though he were walking into a pile of cotton that got denser and denser with every step. When he finally reached the line, he couldn't go over it. His nose touched an invisible wall that seemed to be made of brick, completely impenetrable.

The bishop finally gave up and retreated in a huff, and the grandfather remarked to Ambrose that he should never forget "the old ways." This was one of them, known as "the line of safety." It had long been used in Nigeria by women while they were farming; they would place their babies on the ground and draw a circle around them, which would keep them inside and all the dangers of the bush country outside. His grandfather told him that this had worked for thousands of years until the missionaries came and told the people it wouldn't work. Only then did the line of safety begin failing.

Another story Ambrose told me about his grandfather involved their going into the bush to do medical research. They built a platform four or five feet high next to the river where all the animals came to drink in the evenings. Then, they smeared their bodies with the fat of all the different predators expected at the water hole and climbed to the top of the platform. When the lions and other carnivores arrived, Ambrose told me, "It was as though we were invisible." The animals that surrounded the platform didn't seem to realize that they were being observed by two men lying right above their heads.

During that time, Ambrose and his grandfather would watch unsuccessful kills by the predators and then follow the survivors into the bush, observing the self-treatment practices of the wounded animals. For example, if a jackal was bitten in the leg by a lion, it might go out into the bush, chew up a particular plant, and spit it out on the wound. When that happened, the old man and Ambrose would take a sample of the plant and enter its name into a carefully constructed log, noting that it was the proper plant to use in case of a bite from a lion. Most of the potions used in traditional African medicine have been researched in this manner for thousands of years.

In 1980, I traveled to Africa with Ambrose, with an eye to finding distribution for an album he had recorded at the Church Studio in Tulsa. It was truly one of the most unusual experiences of my life.

Lagos International is a world-class airport by any definition, complete with automatic digital schedules, moving sidewalks, and all the other technologies you would expect from any intercontinental air-travel hub. We had not been there long, though, before we encountered our first obstacle: an immigration officer who wasn't going to let us enter the country because we didn't have our visas in place when we arrived. After being in crowded planes for 12 or 14 hours, I was exhausted and a little short of patience, especially when it looked as though the man was going to make us leave the country.

Then, Ambrose took the official aside. A few minutes later, the man presented us both with new 30-day visitation visas. After we had left him, I asked Ambrose how he'd managed to get us into the country. He told me he had given the man a five-dollar bill, which seemed to have made him "quite happy."

That turned out to be the program for the whole of Nigeria.

At the airport, right outside the immigration doors, we were thrust into a mass of humanity that defies description. And since we had arrived on December 23, every person within speaking distance offered a greeting to "Father Christmas"—who, of course, was yours truly. It was the stuff of science-fiction, arriving in a country I had never before visited, peopled by another race, and being personally greeted as Santa Claus by three or four thousand people over the next few days.

We found a group of taxis right outside the airport and a frenetic discussion began between Ambrose and a cab driver about the cost of the trip we wanted to take. I thought this was a little odd, since the meter was prominently located in the middle of the dashboard, but finally they agreed on a price and we were underway.

The Nigerians seem to have adopted many of the least-desirable components of civilization. When we arrived at our destination, the meter was showing one-third of the agreed-upon price. Later on, when one of my cameramen arrived from L.A. and failed to negotiate the fare with his driver, his life was threatened when he balked at paying $120 for the ride. According to the meter, he owed $8.70.

Another curious phenomenon was the way the Nigerians used their car horns. Whether there was anybody on the road or not, each driver honked about every ten seconds, to sort of announce his or her presence. That made for quite a lot of noise in the middle of Lagos, where there might have been as many as a thousand cars crowded into one small area; the sound was even stranger on a desolated road with no one else in sight.

When we left the airport, we were on a superhighway with six lanes on either side of a tailored median, lined with many sodium lights. After a couple of miles, however, we traveled down an off-ramp that seemed to take us five centuries back in time. The road changed from concrete to dirt, with potholes that were literally larger than our taxi. When we encountered these holes, it was necessary for the cabbie to drive down one side of them and up the other; when we were at the bottom, the road was often higher than the cab's roof. On this road there were no lights anywhere, except for scattered small fires burning among the thousands of residents.

The number of people gathered at any public place in Nigeria makes Manhattan look like Wyoming. A bus stop might have 2,000 people waiting, with buses arriving every five minutes and departing with passengers clinging to the tops and sides and packed inside like sardines.

We traveled for miles before reaching our destination, passing what seemed to be millions of structures about four feet high, principally made from boxes and packing crates, stretching in every direction farther than the eye could see. These were all dwellings where two or more people lived.

Finally, we arrived at our hotel, owned by one of Ambrose's old friends. This was where we intended to stay for the duration of our trip. I got the distinct impression that the rooms there were rented by the hour, primarily to the patrons of the bar that lay just off the lobby. But there was electricity and air-conditioning—the outside temperature never got below 110 while we were there—so I thought we would be comfortable. That was before I realized the electricity and air-conditioning were only on for about one hour a day. Just when you least expected it, the power and cold air would go away and stay gone for 18 hours or so.

On the night of our arrival our hotel host invited us into his air-conditioned office for palm wine. He and Ambrose talked about old times with an abundance of good humor that only increased with the rather substantial wine consumption. At one point, a giant rat ran in to the middle of the floor, frolicking as the visitors watched, the storytelling continuing without any comment about the furry intruder.

Throughout our stay, we were never allowed to leave the hotel compound without guards, who lived outside in the five-car parking area that fronted the hotel. There was much speculation among the locals about how much my head would be worth, given that I was a white man with long white hair. A price in the neighborhood of $25,000 was finally accepted as plausible payment for getting Father Christmas's head into your house for your next ceremony. Other body parts, they told me, wouldn't fetch as much.

When we did depart the hotel, we were stopped constantly by the police. Every time it happened, Ambrose would jump out of the car and announce, "I am Ambrose Campbell," which seemed to make zero impression on any of the policeman. Every time we were detained I was sure we were going to be killed on the spot. They would open our trunk, trying to take whatever was in it for "evidence." It was all very frightening.

One day, a church service was going on directly across the street, and my cameraman took some pictures of it from the hotel balcony. When one of the worshippers noticed this, he became enraged. Soon, his ire spread throughout the congregation, with many people leaving the service to charge across the street and raise their fists in protest. It didn't stop there. That night, they staged a parade, marching back and forth in front of the hotel and playing drums for about an hour, beginning at about 4 a.m. About 70 people were involved in this protest march, which was really quite threatening.

After a few days, when the temperature and unpredictable power outages became unbearable, we moved to the Lagos Holiday Inn, which had electricity all the time but water only about an hour a day. The water, blood-red in color, was brought in on a tanker truck. When the truck arrived, everybody rushed to get a shower before the water was all gone.

The internal phone service of the country was inoperable. It was much easier to call New York than to call the house next door. When we finally did get through to the Lagos airport, we found that all flights out of the country were booked solid. It was so exasperating that I called New York and started pricing charter jets. The quotes ran quite high, but I came very close to putting my $25,000 head on one of them to get out of there. Instead, we went downtown to the ticket office in person to ask about getting reservations. Immediately, they told us all departing flights were full for the next 10 days. But when Ambrose gave the clerk five dollars he suddenly found two seats on an airliner departing the next morning.

Right before we were to board, a man in a black suit approached us. He carried a sawed-off shotgun and a machine pistol, and he hit the airport floor in front of us with much clattering of armament. As he dropped down and kissed Ambrose's feet, he explained that he was head of airport security and, upon recognizing Ambrose, wanted to come over and pay his respects. Luckily, I had worn my brown pants that day.

Incidentally, when we finally got on the flight, it was only half-full.

On another occasion, Ambrose and I visited a Nigerian settlement in North Carolina that had been started by a New Yorker some 27 years earlier. I'd seen a program about it on PBS and was sure it was something Ambrose would find interesting. Since we happened to be in the general area, we were able to locate the encampment after some questioning of the locals.

About 200 people lived there, with many guards and automatic weapons in evidence at the front gate and inside the campground. In fact, the weaponry reminded me of the police in Nigeria. It is pretty amazing that the settlement exists at all in the Deep South, much less with all the armament.

The guards at the gate were not impressed by our request to visit the "king" of the camp, but they finally sent word to him that he had a visitor from Nigeria. Some of the guards were plainly disturbed by our visit and remained that way throughout our stay. Others, however, especially the religious figures, were pleased with the opportunity to visit with a real son of Yoruba.

Once we were let into the encampment, we were taken to the front door of the "castle," a crudely constructed affair made of plywood and tin. Stepping up, Ambrose struck three loud blows on the front door, yelling a Yoruban phrase at the top of his voice. A few second later, a reply in Yoruba came from inside the castle. Two more times, Ambrose struck the door with three blows so hard I thought it might collapse, calling out in his mother tongue. Two more times he was answered from inside.

After the third answer, we entered the building and proceeded to the inner chamber, where the king was located. Seated on his throne, he made polite conversation with Ambrose in Yoruba, obviously enjoying the opportunity to speak to someone so well-informed. The doubtful guards remained so throughout the visit, but the king as well as the priests around him became more excited as the conversation went on.

Following the meeting between the king and Ambrose, we were taken on a complete tour of the village, which included many Yoruba shrines and altars as well as dance arenas and food-preparation areas that were identical to those in a Nigerian village. Upon seeing some of the religious shrines, Ambrose began to joyfully explain to the expatriated New Yorker king all the meanings and significances of the various artifacts that were on display. At one point, he grabbed a statue and another artifact and changed their locations, explaining the error of placement to the king and how it adversely affected the spirituality. It made me a little nervous, but the king was greatly pleased and only the guards remained skeptical.

Feeling like an invisible fly on the wall, I listened as the bond between the king and his Nigerian visitor strengthened. The king explained to Ambrose how he had become unhappy with his life in New York City and vowed to move to North Carolina and establish a village that would be based on the heritage that had been denied him, since he was the descendant of slaves. He'd done a remarkable job. Yoruba was not only spoken exclusively at the encampment; it was also taught to the many children there by the king and his six wives. Much attention was paid to the old religions and the ways that life played out in Nigeria in an earlier time.

When we finally left, I felt that the people of the village had been grateful for the opportunity to talk with a true priest from Yorubaland.

Whether its because of his Nigerian upbringing or something else entirely, Ambrose Campbell doesn't worry about much when it comes to people. I once dropped him off in Harlem because he wanted to "look around," and I didn't see him for more than three days. I was more than a little worried. When he finally returned, I asked him what had happened.

He said that after I had left him, he immediately went up to the biggest, meanest-looking man he could find on the street, gave him all his money, and said, "I am from out of town. Would you be so good as to protect me and show me around a little bit?" Within the hour, he was speaking to an audience of 300 Black Panthers, trying to convince them that violence was not the answer. He spent the next three days as a guest in private homes and in many different centers of culture in the area. At the end of the visitation, his guide and protector returned all of his money. Others had picked up his expenses. He reported that it had been a most enjoyable tour of Harlem.

Ambrose Campbell performs with Russell in a 1979 Tulsa show. Born Oladipupo Adekoya Campbell in Lagos, Nigeria, he has been called the father of modern Nigerian music. After meeting Campbell in 1972, Russell began using him as a percussionist in his touring bands, calling him his spiritual advisor. Their personal and professional relationship lasted until Campbell's death in 2006.

Photo by Steve Todoroff. Courtesy of the Oklahoma Museum of Popular Culture/Steve Todoroff Collection.

Chapter Fifteen

A HOUSE IS NOT

FOR A TIME I was living in a small fishing cabin on the Grand Lake O' the Cherokees, about seventy miles northeast of Tulsa. It was part of a picturesque and primitive little resort that featured floating motel rooms with boat parking right inside. Originally called Pappy Reeves' Floating Motel, it was my home while my house and studio were being built on the property.

■■ ■■■

When Leon Russell was a sophomore at Will Rogers High School, he had very short hair with a widow's peak and he had what one of his elders described as "a silly grin."

Nobody dreamed then that he would grow up to be a super rock star with the means to build a half million dollar recording studio overlooking Grand Lake . . . .

Russell bought the best quality microphones and speakers and his U-shaped control board is called "amazing." It was custom made for him in England and is seven feet wide.

When Russell is not recording, the studio will be used by others including Bob Dylan and George Harrison, associates say. Another rock star who will record at the studio is J.J. Cale. . . .

—from "Rock Star Building $500,000 Lake Retreat" by Joanne Gordon in the July 30, 1972 Tulsa Sunday World.

The caretakers who came with the property were F.M. and Lola Watson, a beautiful old couple who worked there for me for a couple of years before retiring and moving into town. Lola was quite a talker and storyteller in her own right. One day, when I was returning from a speedboat cruise with Bob Dylan, Lola came up with glasses of iced tea and spoke to Bob: "You know," she said, pointing at me, "this guy here is famous all over the world." Bob smiled and shared her enthusiastic astonishment at this fact.

▪▪ ▪▪▪

When I was there Leon was recording Freddie King, or Willie [Nelson] or somebody, and we had been up for three days straight. I had been in bed an hour and a half when Leon came in and woke me up. He said that I had to get up, and I said, "Why?"

He said, "Because my friend Bob Dylan's here."

It was Bob Dylan, Harry Dean Stanton, [and] a guy called Larry who was Bob's only friend left over from [his] high-school days in Minnesota. They were in an old two-door burned-up '68 Chevy. There were two Mexican guys who helped Larry because he was a quadriplegic in a wheelchair. They just showed up, and how the fuck they ever found the place I'll never know.

—Emily Smith, *from a January 29, 1989 interview with Brian Thompson*

▪▪ ▪▪▪

After the studio was finished, I cut several albums there, including *O'Neal Twins*, with a gospel duo, which came out on Shelter; a couple of Freddie King albums; and most of the *Carney* album. I also used the studio as a rehearsal room for many tours of that period.

▪▪ ▪▪▪

Editors' note: Since Carney—*which included Leon's first Top 40 single, "Tight Rope"—was released by Shelter in June of 1972, Leon was apparently recording at the Grand Lake studio before the* Tulsa World *article appeared. The Freddie King LPs he mentions are 1972's* The Texas Cannonball *and 1973's* Woman Across the River, *two of three (with 1971's* Getting Ready*) King discs to bear the Shelter imprint.*

The O'Neal Twins, Edgar and Edward, were an established African-American duo out of St. Louis. Their 1974 O'Neal Twins *album was Shelter's first foray into the gospel market.*

■■ ■■■

After I moved to Tulsa, the Grand Lake property was in disuse to a great extent and a friend of mine came up with the idea of turning it into a commercial operation. Although I felt that the property was worth about a half-million dollars at the time, I offered to sell him a half-interest for $100,000, to be paid out of his share of income from the commercial enterprise. He accepted.

After about 10 months had elapsed with no evidence of any commerce, I informed him I could no longer afford to keep the property and was going to donate the entire estate to Oral Roberts University, which was located in Tulsa. Further, I was going to give him and his wife $12,000 for their effort and expenses on the commercial project. They had reported expenditures of about $5,000.

As I was in the last stages of the transfer of the property to the university, I was served with a document called a *caveat emptor*. This little epistle stated that I had sold them half the property and that it was only worth $200,000 at the time, the logic being that $100,000 was therefore half its value. They didn't remember anything about having to buy their half of the property out of income generated by the commercial enterprise.

Also, since the property had just been appraised at almost $500,000, they wanted their $100,000—which hadn't been paid—for their half, along with half the difference between $200,000 and $500,000 dollars, using the theory of "unjust enrichment." In other words, what they were saying was that my giving away to charity the property that they had spent $5,000 on and—by their argument—increasing its value by $300,000 was unjustly enriching me.

Needless to say, the judge didn't buy that idea. He awarded them about $1,500 less than their reported expenditures, saying their accounting was inflated and unreasonable. Keeping in mind that I had offered them $12,000, that figure was about $8,000 less than they would've gotten from me in the first place.

To add insult to injury, they appealed the case, and when it finally came to trial in Denver, Colorado, they were awarded another $1,200.

I think all my legal fees for this fiasco didn't even amount to $100,000. It was sort of like paying for the dental work on a gift horse.

I enjoyed very much the time I lived at the lake house. It all started as a remodel of the buildings associated with Pappy Reeves' Floating Motel, but it ended up as a beautiful seven-bedroom house, cantilevered over the water, with two separate guest houses, a large studio, and an enclosed swimming pool and greenhouse.

One night as I was getting ready to leave on tour, Emily happened to mention that there was a beautiful house on the market at 24th Place in Tulsa, meant to be one-of-a-kind. I drove by the place at 10 o'clock at night, and being unable to make an appointment to see it at that time made an offer without going in—just on the basis of seeing the outside. This was during the real-estate depression of 1973, and my offer was half the asking price. Nevertheless, after just a few days they told me it had been accepted.

Although I was very anxious to see the inside, I was on the road continually for the next two months. Finally, when I was playing in El Paso and had only two days off before the next show, I rented a plane and flew through the worst storm I had ever experienced to get to Tulsa for a look. It was well worth the trouble.

After being inside the house for about ten minutes, I was standing in the ballroom when I suddenly remembered that I had played a graduation party there for Trish McClintock when I was in high school. I recalled playing the piano at that affair, looking at all the magnificent wood paneling and wondering what kind of people lived in places like this one. When I was a teenager, my family lived on Tulsa's north side in a considerably more modest housing addition; the home I was standing in was the only house on the more expensive south side I had ever been in at the time. It was at that party that I'd first tasted cocktail shrimp, which had been served on a huge tray with plenty of ice and sauce. The opulence I remembered was overwhelming.

Fifteen years later, the home was in quite a different condition. The magnificent wood paneling, as I later found out, was covered with 11 coats of paint of various garish colors. All the paint was removed, back down to the original wood, with little trouble, except for the fire that started when one of the workers dragged his steel wool over a live electrical outlet, igniting the paint remover that covered a large section of the walls. The only good thing about it was that insurance provided enough funds to completely redecorate the entire smoke-damaged house.

I had bad luck with fires in that place. When I was living there with Mary, we asked an employee to get rid of some wasps that were nesting near the front porch. He took it upon himself to make a torch to hold up to the nest, which he thought would "smoke out" the insects. The massive crown moulding that ran completely around the outside of the house had been designed as a ventilation system, and when the torch was brought near it, the fire was sucked inside. Within a few seconds, our top floor was ablaze.

As it turned out, the fire only damaged one of the upstairs rooms, but the water used to put it out ran all through the house and ultimately down to the studio, completely ruining all the bottom floors. It was so depressing that we moved out, first to an apartment and, later, to California. We never lived in the house again.

After a few years, the place was bought by an enterprising developer, who managed to turn it into four houses, demolishing the original home before the neighborhood historical-preservation committee could get wind of his plans.

■■ ■■■

Firemen inspect damage from a fire Sunday in the home of recording star Leon Russell, 1151 E. 24th Place. The blaze gutted a third-floor room and caused some smoke and water damage to the home's interior, officials said. Dist. Chief Hal Warnock said there were no injuries from the fire, which apparently was started by a torch being used to burn off wasp nests from below the roof eaves.

—photo caption from October 11, 1976 Tulsa World

Rock music star Leon Russell, a longtime Tulsan, is selling his Maple Ridge house and moving to California.

Professional movers had taken all of Russell's belongings out of his house at 1151 E. 24ᵗʰ Place Saturday. Spokesmen said the house would be offered for sale by a Realtor.

Movers said the furniture would be sent to California, but they did not know the location. Russell has maintained a residence in Encino, Calif., near Los Angeles.

Russell could not be reached for comment.

Russell had a recording studio in the basement of his Tulsa residence, and also formerly owned a studio at 312 S. Trenton Ave., in a building that once was a church. . . .

Spokesmen said security guards will be posted at the former residence.

—"Leon Russell Leaving Tulsa," unbylined story in the March 14, 1977 Tulsa Tribune

■■ ■■■

I had so much junk to move from Tulsa to Encino that it made the cover of a trade magazine for household movers. The article inside was titled "The Largest Residential Move in History." A big garage sale would have been a good idea, especially since the Tulsa house had about 10,000 square feet and the one in Encino was around 3,500. Plus, I had my extensive tape library and studio equipment to deal with. Eventually, I found a large warehouse in California and used it to store everything in large stacked rows until I could get a chance to relocate it or dispose of it in some other way. I bought the building from the man who had allegedly sponsored and created the original version of the television show *Let's Make A Deal*, invented specifically as an outlet for his appliance store.

Our home in Encino was just off Ventura Boulevard. Originally built by Bud Abbott of the famed comedy team Abbott & Costello, it was a rambling ranch affair that had once been surrounded by a large orange grove, back when that part of the San Fernando Valley was a rural area. I soundproofed the living room and two bedrooms, using one bedroom for drums and the other for a control room. Most of the two duet albums I did with Mary were recorded there.

■■ ■■■

Editors' note: By this time, the Shelter Records partnership with Denny Cordell had dissolved. Leon's two duet albums with Mary, 1976's The Wedding Album *and 1977's* Make Love to the Music, *were released on his own Paradise label, distributed by Warner Bros. Records.*

■■ ■■■

The warehouse I had bought became Studio A, as well as the business offices of Paradise Records and Video. My deal with Warners was substantially funded, enabling me to build an impressive video facility. Unfortunately, MTV wasn't even on the drawing board at that time and record companies were not convinced that video was very important in record merchandising. For Warner Brothers to be interested in any kind of video at that time, an act would have to sell 700,000 units.

I was asked to be on a video-conference panel, held at Universal Studios, that dealt with the future of the record business and how television might have an effect on it. I couldn't believe the attitude reflected in the questions asked by the audience. There seemed to be no one in attendance who thought that television had any connection with the sale of records.

One person asked me, "If video is such an important merchandising tool for records, why aren't the big stars using it?"

At that time, via a TV promotion, Kenny Rogers had sold seven million copies of a greatest-hits collection, previously available in stores, in a period of six weeks. Slim Whitman, Boxcar Willie, Ted Turner, and MTV were yet to come.

Russell's Paradise Studio and Compound, near Tia Juana, Oklahoma, on the Grand Lake of the Cherokees, circa 1971. Following the formation of Shelter Records, Russell's new partner and manager, Denny Cordell, advised him to "leave behind the debauchery of Los Angeles" and move back to his home state. Russell took the advice, and in late 1970 bought a historic mansion in Tulsa, a church building that he converted to a recording studio and Shelter's Tulsa headquarters, and this piece of property, complete with a floating fishing dock, swimming pool, and, soon, a state-of-the-art studio. It was located about an hour's drive northeast of Tulsa.

The Grand Lake complex became a getaway for Russell, where he could relax and record himself and other artists. Those who availed themselves of the Paradise Studio included Bob Seger, Freddie King, George Jones, Jon Anderson, and gospel act the O'Neal Twins.

Filmmaker Les Blank shot footage at the compound from 1972 through 1974 for the documentary *A Poem Is A Naked Person.*

Russell ultimately donated the property to Oral Roberts University in Tulsa.

Photo by R.C. Bradley. Courtesy of the Oklahoma Museum of Popular Culture/ Steve Todoroff Collection.

Russell's Tulsa mansion, which he purchased in July 1972. Originally built by L.E.Z. Aaronson, the patriarch of one of Tulsa's pioneering families, it was located it the prestigious Maple Ridge section of the city—relatively close to the new Tulsa headquarters of Shelter Records. After purchasing it, he realized he had played a debutante ball there while in high school.

As was the case with his former place on Skyhill Drive, Russell wasted little time in building a home studio for his new house.

Photo by Steve Todoroff. Courtesy of the Oklahoma Museum of Popular Culture/ Steve Todoroff Collection.

Chapter Sixteen

THE LIVE SHOWS

FOR ABOUT A two-year period [circa 1980-81], I played with the New Grass Revival, a fantastic bluegrass-type band that included Sam Bush on mandolin and fiddle, John Cowan on bass, Curtis Burch on acoustic guitar, and Courtney Johnson on the banjo, with either Ambrose or Bill Kenner playing beaded gourd. It was a most enjoyable and unusual period for me, as I played a lot of different kinds of venues and discovered a different strata of musical performance. Many times we would take out our instruments in the waiting areas of airports, or rest areas along the highway, and play for a couple of hours. Since we didn't need electricity, we could play just about anywhere. We would pass an automobile junkyard and Sam would say, "There's a bluegrass festival. Let's stop and play."

Kathy Bush, Liz Cowan, and Hazel Johnson, the wives, were our roadies. It was a different kind of road show.

When the Revival and I went to Australia with the Amazing Rhythm Aces, the audiences in most cases would sort of stand around the auditoriums in shock when they saw there were no drums or big amplifiers in our stage setup. But eventually, the New Wave kids would come up to the stage and start doing their pogo-type dancing, and the crowds would slowly come around.

Singing with Sam and John was a real treat for me. I was not used to singing in a trio and it was completely effortless. All I had to do was sing the lead, and they would anticipate the harmony and phrasing, seemingly by intuition.

We did one TV show together, a concert that produced a live album [*Leon Russell & New Grass Revival—the Live Album*, released in
1981 on Paradise Records] at Perkins Palace in Pasadena, California.
After I left the band, Courtney and Curtis were replaced with Bela
Fleck and Pat Flynn, and the group was just on the verge of gaining
national when it disbanded [in 1990]. Seeing that was a disappoint-
ment for me, but after twenty years I suppose there were other rows
to hoe. Sam is currently playing with Emmylou Harris, Bela has his
own band, The Flecktones, and John is pursuing a solo career in rock.

For a few years, I had a band with Edgar Winter that was also very
enjoyable. Edgar is a master musician I first saw at the Hollywood
Bowl with his brother, Johnny. I wasn't really aware of him until that
time, but I was very impressed, as he played all the "Fathead" Newman
alto saxophone parts, sang all the Margie Hendrix parts, and played
all the organ parts on their versions of the Ray Charles numbers they
played that evening.

■■ ■■■

*[Editors' note: Hendrix was the leader of Ray Charles's Raelettes, famed
for her powerful voice, while David "Fathead" Newman was a noted jazz
and R&B saxophonist who played brief but memorable leads on several
of Charles's early records.]*

■■ ■■■

I remember thinking at the time that someday I would really like
to be able to work with him.

We later played a couple of shows together with our bands, and
I took that opportunity to ask him to sit in on alto sax. He is so proficient that it was an effortless meld. When we finally started playing
together all the time I would occasionally get complaints that I was
not doing enough, but it was such a pleasure to sit back, be in the
band, and watch Edgar do his thing.

■■ ■■■

It was . . . a show that defied categorization, a rock show with jazz-fusion overtones that called up the past without repeating it. With Winter—dressed in a multicolored body suit that made him look like a psychedelic leprechaun—fronting the band, the concert soon settled into the musical equivalent of a tag-team match. First Winter would take the spotlight with a song, then Leon, then Winter again. And so it went, Winter with the likes of "Fly Away" and the radio hits ["Frankenstein," "Free Ride"] . . . Leon countering with everything from "Over the Rainbow" and "Rollin' in My Sweet Baby's Arms" to "A Song for You." In a three-song set with only Winter (on saxophone and vocals) and Russell on stage, Winter even sang one of Russell's most famous tunes, "This Masquerade." . . . .

There are those, this writer among them, who miss the sublime sounds that Russell can coax out of a grand piano, rather than the electronic keyboard he had with him Sunday night. There were probably also those who would've liked a bit more of Leon. But the show was well-played and well-received—for, perhaps, its, and Russell's timelessness, as much as anything else.

—from an August 8, 1988 Tulsa World *review by John Wooley*

■■ ■■■

Edgar and I played a successful tour of Brazil, also going to Russia for a couple of concerts. The trip to Russia was a revelation about political systems that don't quite give enough regard to human nature. It must have seemed like a good idea at the time to Mr. Lenin and the other political architects, but the resulting landscape was a wasteland that seemed to be made up of components from both Washington, D.C. and Paraguay. We saw miles of empty storefronts with vacant plate-glass display cases along with literally thousands of buildings built in the style of the Treasury Department or similar D.C. structures. The hotel where we stayed had 5,000 rooms, but the carpets looked as though the Hell's Angels had come through and changed their oil there.

The hotel restaurant offered bad wieners and green peas for breakfast every day. The maids and other members of the staff clamored for our leftover food, soap, and toilet paper; when we contributed these items as we were leaving, they looked as though they had been given gold. The generic tissue offered in the toilets of Russia looks and feels a little like our waxed paper used to wrap leftover food. Please don't squeeze the Charmin.

After visiting the Kremlin and some of the old cathedrals, I got the impression that Russia had been a country peopled with a colorful race of gypsies who had been conquered sometime in the past by an adversary. That adversary had then turned the whole country into a failing enterprise run by a centralized bureaucratic government—sort of like what might happen in the United States Postal Service took over Ted Turner's companies. I couldn't help thinking what miracles could be wrought by Sam Walton, or even someone like Colonel Sanders, in terms of distributing food and other bare essentials to the Russian people.

It was very strange indeed to go into stores and have Russian currency refused in favor or American dollars or German marks, the signs proclaiming "Hard Currency Only." Apparently, the problem is one of distribution, since the highways all turn into dirt roads about 50 miles outside of Moscow. The American interstate-highway system that originated about 25 years ago as an arm of the defense network has, whether by accident or design, been a saving grace to goods distribution in our country.

On the other end of the scale is Japan. I recently played a series of concerts there and was constantly aware I was in a country with a higher standard of living than my own. Luxury cars not even imported to the USA lined the streets everywhere. In Japan, it is against the law to drive a car with a dent or some other cosmetically disfiguring condition; the police will give tickets or impound vehicles for this infraction as quickly as they will for speeding or overdue registration. I sometimes feel that Japan may have won WW II after all.

I remarked to one of my friends over there that I hoped the promoter was making money on the tour, since one of the clubs had only 600 seats. He pointed out that the ticket range for that engagement was $45-65 and both shows were sold out.

There is a lot of money in Japan.

Chapter Seventeen

WILLIE AND ME

I **FIRST MET WILLIE** [in the early '70s] when he attended one of my concerts in Houston. After the show, he came backstage, bringing some truly Jamaican-sized joints for my approval. We talked about the show and he told me that his daughter had introduced him to my recordings with Delaney & Bonnie and Joe Cocker. Both of us had a good time, and he decided to come to my show the next night in Albuquerque, New Mexico.

At that time, Willie was traveling with his entire band in a small motor home. Times were a little tough for him. I started coming to shows he was doing in places like the John T. Floore Country store in Helotis, Texas, where the cowboys were asked to remove their hats before entering the building. Until then, I'd never realized how emasculating that can be for a range rover.

Right before he got his deal with Atlantic Records, he came to Nashville with me when I was cutting "If I Were A Carpenter" at Pete Drake's studio. We also cut a couple of good songs on Willie at that time. Later, we did a television show at Johnny Cash's studio, The House of Cash, in Hendersonville, Tennessee. Many stars turned out to help us with that, including Bill Monroe, Earl Scruggs, Ernest Tubb, Jeanne Pruett, and Roy Acuff, and many stories were told about the early days of country music. This came along sometime after my first Hank Wilson album, and I think many of the country stars were curious to see this rock 'n' roll guy who had made a country record. Most of the musicians who'd played on the Hank Wilson sessions were there for the television show. Unfortunately, we had some audio problems and the show was never completed or edited.

Willie and I did another show together, taped during the making of the *One for the Road* LP [released in 1979]. I was in the process of building my Paradise Video studios out in California, and much of the new TV equipment was still being unpacked as we were shooting the show. Consequently, we didn't have time to check it all out before putting it to use. This resulted in a faulty sync generator—the equipment that kept the seven tape machines running exactly together—and many hundreds of hours of trying to match the time codes for all the machines. We didn't really succeed, and the show suffered for it.

During the tapings, all the available parking in my neighborhood for six blocks in any direction was taken up by members of our cast and production crew, which made the neighbors quite unhappy. When this situation progressed into a second week, they reported me to the city for operating a business in a residential area. In Los Angeles this is quite a serious charge. However, by the time the inspector arrived on the scene the project had been over for a couple of weeks, and he just complimented me on my house and left.

As I wrote earlier, I built a video and audio recording studio in a former warehouse on Magnolia Boulevard in Burbank, which also housed the Paradise Records and Video offices. The Paradise Video project was ahead of its time. Since there was no MTV then, nor any other outlets of that type, it was difficult to merchandise video. Pay-cable services were just getting started, and Ted Turner's broadcast empire lay in the future, so the regular networks and their local affiliates were about the only possible markets.

My idea was to do a television series called *The Paradise Show*, which would be shot and broadcast weekly from Burbank or some remote location out on the road. I successfully built the equipment to do it, but because of my divorce and the massive problems with the first show I tried, the one with Willie, I never really got the result I was after. Disappointed, I finally gave up and moved to Nashville, Tennessee.

By that time, I was tired of L.A.

Russell and Willie Nelson, seen here during a 1984 video shoot in Los Colinas, Texas. In the early '70s, not long after the two superstars had first made contact with one another, they were listening to some of Nelson's early recordings for Liberty when Russell realized he'd been on those sessions. The pair remained very close until Russell's death.

Photo by Steve Todoroff. Courtesy of the Oklahoma Museum of Popular Culture/Steve Todoroff Collection.

THE LEON RUSSELL
MONUMENT FUND SUPPORTERS

WE LOST LEON RUSSELL on November 13, 2016, and to honor his memory a committee was formed to raise funds to build a monument headstone for Leon's cremains at Memorial Park Cemetery in Tulsa, Oklahoma. Almost $50,000 was raised to purchase a burial estate and the black granite monument stone, which was unveiled and dedicated on November 11, 2018.

The family of Leon Russell & the Leon Russell Monument Committee wish to thank the following people who made donations or otherwise supported the Leon Russell Monument Fund. Thanks to you, we were able to reach our goal and make the monument at Memorial Park Cemetery in Tulsa, Oklahoma a reality.

Natalie Pagano

Kathi L. Wakefield-Trimble

Leslie Goodwin

Deborah Miller

John McDonnell

Brian & Soraya Thompson

Richard & Jemma Pfenniger, Jr.

Debbie K. Brassfield

Steffanie & Gary Busey

William G. Avery

Constance S. Ryder

Sandra Weinfield

Jim & Minisa Halsey

Dr. F.J. Huskey, Inc.

Kathy & Steve Todoroff

Debbie Todoroff

Jeff Moore

Dr. Bob Blackburn

OKPOP

Larry O'Dell

Elizabeth Matz

Linda McGrath

Jackie & Jim Karstein

Chris Klein-Goss

Rhea Dawson

Sandy DeMartini

David E Hannah

Randy Lowen

Karen Eberstein-Guidry

Barbara Hogan Daniels

Rose Annette Banks

Linda & Robert Blanck

Larry Fennell

Nita & Gary Sissell

Tom Zizzi

Linda J. Keene

Robert Lischke

Lisa J. Stearns

Mary Nell Shiflet

Mary Jo & Gailard Sartain

Bob & Debbie Cox

David Schram

John Dickinson

Steve Burns

Memorial Park Cemetery

Darlene Carradine

Ronnie Felts

Cindy Gibson

Nick Schneider

Joey Findley

Nancy Deere

Joyce Hulet

Rebecca Jennings

Pam Bradford

Jerri Hemphill

Nancy Barnum

Robert Susswein

Rebecca Bilbrey

Nan Wall Hay

Reba Whisenhunt

Jean Manning

Lisa Volm

Linda Marshall

Michelle Hayslip

Kena Keith

Gaile M. Farmer

Cheryl Beddow

Cheryl Batten

Janet Manno

Jerry Wormington

Karen White

Christina Bowles

Bonnie Beards
William J. Duensing
Rhonda Miller
Leigh Melton Hancock
Dale Fleming
Rosemary Walters
Mena Paulson
Rowena Wilson
Gary & Debbie Persing
Raymond Etheredge
Betsy Smith
Teresa Knox
Donna J. Mathews
Rob Kirk
Dawn Buss
Richard Willis
Carol Peters
Russell Reeves
Winnie Owen Kostainsek
William E. Wilson
Carole Cleveland
Beverely Diorio
Becca Glaser
Randy Smith
Seneca McIntosh
Jodi Cash
Ronald O'Connor
Charles Shipley
Susan Carlson
John Wooley
Anita Justus
Susan Clark
Robert O. Sadler
Becky Ford
Robert Wentland
Greg Neffle

Maxine Imanaba
Circle Cinema
Jan & Dwight Twilley
Sarah Hart
Thomas & Dee Ann Ekis
Blank Family Trust
Harrod Blank
Les Blank Films, Inc.
Wanona Cass
Alanna Nash
Deborah Meek
Crystal Longdon
Steve Burnett
Teri Walline
Alan Knox
Becki Jennings
Connie Watkins Hodges
Elizabeth Pennock
Edna Reeves
Laura Tait
Mardi Murcek
74 Shades of Leon
T.M. Harcrow
Doug Pepper
Deborah Peel
Sarai & Howard Aleshire
Lois Mullin
R. Scott Phillips
Kathleen Davis
Lori R. Call
David Boddie
Patricia Story
Donna Wood
Laurie Foster
Bill Stanford
Rob & Linda Blanck

Nancy Murphy

Linda DeWitt

Cathleen Doyle

Lucia Ruta

Michael Shema

Sally Mathews

Stella Austin

Joe Land

Susan Williams

Rick Huskey

Deann Beach

Dominic Bertini

Millard Pickering

Candice McDaniel

Mandy Robert

Century City Artist Corp

Barbara Coward

Bradley Dede

Sally Hensley

Michael Broyles

Nancy Robinson

Roger Freeman

Jane Whitaker

Liz Bentson

Lisa Riggs

Mark Milberger

Carrie Lindsay

Stan Irick

Michelle Owens

Larry Gregory

Robert Koury

James Kyzer

Janet Giambattista

Diana Green

Janet Manno

William Avery

John Gorse

Elton John Charitable Fund

Sir Elton John

Jon Howard

Stuart Taylor

Cain's Concert Fundraiser

The Bohans

Brad & Amy Absher

Debra Roberts

Etta Meyer Parsons

Marlyn Rose

Ric Olsen

Roger Wyatt

Knoel Honn

Dana Sebek

Jerry & Jennifer Smith

Skip & Patsy Graves

Todd Chapman

Judy Johnson

Jim R. Felts

Kyle McGuire

Jo Ferguson

Philip Ramsey

Tim Connor

Steve & Cinthy Fisher

Rose Mankowski

Scott Merrell

Carol J. Palmer

Bruce Davidson

Christopher Stevens

Steve Liddycoat

Debi Burns

Alan Unell

Linda Brothers

Arlene Ross

Tammy Ramsey

Robyn Smith
Annie Walker
Allison Chaplin
Emily Priddy
Ron Warnick
Georgia Koontz
Valerie Roy
Barbara Burke
Keith Gordon
Arnie Points
Cynthia Ryan
Linda & Will Leiss
Leona Guzowski
Carolyn Walker
Ron, Tonya & Honey Colburn
Robin Guzman
Debra Seifer
John Paddock
Jennalee Foree
Gary Stevenson
Vailia Davidson
Mary Huff
Kyle McGuire
Skipper & Lisa Bain
Wes Bain
Deby Rake
Judy Johnson
Sally Ferguson
Kathleen D'Eramo
Kristofer Olofsson
Janice Roach
Cory Franklin
Chuck Foxen
Stephanie LaFevers
Clark Weins
David Kimball

Mikel Lomsky
Michael Davita
Jon Fahr
Caleb Trowbridge
Scott Musick
Tom Ferrier
Bria & Joey Guns
S. Preece
Mark Hodge
Jo Ferguson
Mychel Matthews
Stephen Walker
Susan Terrana
Jennifer Stokes
Roxnne Harpe
Thomas Pack
Bobbie Bousky
Roy Fontaine
Jean Ann Wright
Barbara Briscoe Perry
Judy VanLandingham-Copeland
James McKillip
Nancy Frazier-Neidhart
Paul Heyman
Stephanie Fox
Diana Lawrence
Peta Byrne
Rosemary O'Donnell
Jason Newsom
Scott Worth
Michael Cimino-Cary
Bryan Huling
Suzanne Stafford
Jonny Wright
Reggie Stafford
Elvis Ripley

Jodi Cash
Crystal Longdon
Jennifer & Roy Attaway
Clifton Sartin
Angelene Ripley Wright
Dori Jungklaus
Ricky & Lydia Moon
Cheryl Thompson
Micky & David Hannah
Dorothy Wright
Mike Hammett
Sue Predis
Debbie Milam
Jeffery Haas
Steve & Charlene Ripley
Mark Blaskovich
Beau & Lyndsi Charron
Brandon Holder
Jack Wessel
Sherman Oaks
Jim Millaway
Jan & Dwight Twilley
Rick & Debbie Hill
John Sires
Pete Serratte
Dylan Harrison Holmes
Peter Thomsen
Bob Stewart
Tim Connelly
Linda Unterreiner
Gordon Holmes
Cynthia Threlkeld
Bill Cox
Constance Wong
Bill Love
Ty Kernea

Debbie Brassfield
Lauren Mitchell
Laura Powel
Sarah Thompson
Susie Que
Richard Eller
Chris Herr
Aleksey Anikeev
Deana Drake
Sandy DeMartini
Brian Rusk
Donnie Benson
Kit Bibee
Sandy DeMartini
Gerald Hetland
Trish McAlpine-Ellis
Sharon Nader
Patricia Turner Custard
Dawn Marie High-Fecher
Margaret Powell
Steven Cox
Marijana Praznik
Anita Justus
Linda Horton
Ron Sheets
Sam Bradshaw
Hal G. Brown
Alex Legg
Sunee Casey
Kim Francis
Mary Lib Stine
Jill Carroll
Shane Roginski
Karen Rodgers
Susie Phillips
Buddy Naylor

Delilah Popplewell
Darrell Mahone
Nick Coby
Judi Moon Dittus
Paul Arrington
Roger Wyatt
Megumi Noguchi
Bonnie Leighty
Rick L. Lane
Bill Thompson
Gaile Farmer
Barbara Andrews
P. McAlpine-Ellis
John Boydston
Patti Oden
Glen Mitchell
Joseph (Cooper) Lake (Young)
Laurie Mason
Greg Gray
David Kors
Louis Herthum
Beverley Halterman

Rich Halstrom
Patricia Layton
Todd Daugherty
Thomas Kelsey
Gregory Brown
Valerie Edwards
Lea Ann Fessenden
Joyce Budd
Lindon Curtis
Kim Hendrickson
Linda Williams
Kyla Huget
Ron Grosland
Gary Thayer
Kim Goldman
Nancy Redfield
Martha Walker
Dennis Wilburn
Brand Knox
Mike Phillips
Betty Hazelton
Eileen Smith

Once in a lifetime across your lifeline crosses an energy
unlike no other. This is Leon Russell to me.

Ultimately planned for the utility of one thing—
the generation of heat under the umbrella of music,
color, and movement.

Leon is an enricher of disguises, a player and master
of consciously-created psychodrama, built upon
a platform of emotional reactions and releases
to stimulate and condition.

Together we've shared the excitement and adventure
of experience both near and far, and once connected
to an energy such as this, it lives forever.

This is the man who taught me the meaning
of anthropology and tourism and that Junior Walker
is like "inventing a vegetable".

May he ride on the back of a catfish into the rainbow spray
of clean Tennessee water to the tune of his choice.

—GARY BUSEY

STEVE TODOROFF, a longtime friend of Leon Russell, has spent decades researching Russell and his musical legacy. Along the way, he's collected a vast amount of Leon memorabilia, as well as many other Tulsa-related items. Recently, he and his wife, Kathy, donated more than 4,500 pieces from this collection to the Oklahoma Museum of Popular Culture (OKPOP), which will be based in Tulsa. Those who've benefited from Steve's comprehensive knowledge of Leon and his work include director Cameron Crowe, the Rock and Roll Hall of Fame, and Sir Elton John. Currently, Steve and John Wooley are working on another book together, tentatively titled *Longhair Music: The Leon Russell Story.*

JOHN WOOLEY, the first writer to be inducted into the Oklahoma Music Hall of Fame, has been writing about the state's music and musicians for well over 30 years. His most recent books include the as-told-to baseball biography *Right Down The Middle: The Ralph Terry Story; Fantasies in the Sand* (with Michael H. Price), a celebration of the Beach Party movie culture; and *Seventh Sense (with Robert A. Brown),* the first novel in an epistolary horror trilogy.

CPSIA information can be obtained
at www.ICGtesting.com
Printed in the USA
LVHW080800290819
628849LV00004B/11/P